THE **FIRST**100**CHORDS**
FOR**PIANO**

How to Learn and Play Piano Chords – The Complete Guide for Beginners

ANGELA**MARSHALL**

FUNDAMENTAL**CHANGES**

The First 100 Chords for Piano

How to Learn and Play Piano Chords – The Complete Guide for Beginners

ISBN: 978-1-78933-383-1

Published by **www.fundamental-changes.com**

Copyright © 2022 Angela Marshall

The moral right of this author has been asserted.

Join our free Facebook Community of Cool Musicians

www.facebook.com/groups/fundamentalguitar

Tag us for a share on Instagram: **FundamentalChanges**

Cover Image Copyright: Shutterstock, SunnyGraph

Contents

Get the Audio

The audio files for this book are available to download for free from **www.fundamental-changes.com.** The link is in the top right-hand corner. Simply select this book title from the drop-down menu and follow the instructions to get the audio.

We recommend that you download the files directly to your computer, not to your tablet, and extract them there before adding them to your media library. You can then put them on your tablet, iPod or burn them to CD. On the download page there is a help PDF and we also provide technical support via the contact form.

For over 350 free guitar lessons with videos check out:

www.fundamental-changes.com

Join our free Facebook Community of Cool Musicians

www.facebook.com/groups/fundamentalguitar

Tag us for a share on Instagram: **FundamentalChanges**

Introduction to the Piano

The chords and techniques in this book will allow you to play most of the songs that you hear on the radio and can be applied to pop, rock, jazz, blues, hip hop, country, and even classical music. These chords will also allow you to write your own songs and arrangements, accompany singers, and play in a band.

In this section you're going to learn the basics of the piano. You'll need to know these concepts to play the exercises in the book, so review this material and come back to this page as needed and use it as a reference.

Let's get started!

Piano music is written on the *grand staff,* which is simply the treble clef and bass clef joined by a bracket.

Don't worry if you don't read music, all the examples include the letter names of each note to make them easier for you to read.

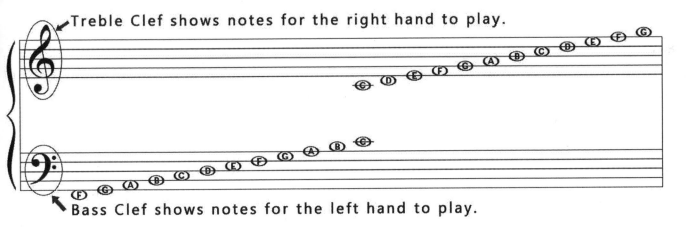

The notes and piano keys are named after the first seven letters of the alphabet and the same pattern of notes repeats across the entire keyboard. You can use the groups of black keys as landmarks to identify the letter names of white keys. For example, the note C is always just to the left of the group of two black keys.

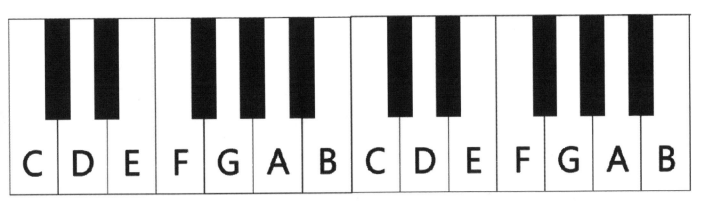

To identify which fingers to use, we give each one a number. Your thumbs are always number one. From there, move outwards and count up to your pinkie which is number five. Numbering the fingers lets us communicate clearly about which fingers to use on each key.

The following chart shows you how to read the rhythms in this book.

Listen to the included audio example. Clap and count along to get a feel for the different rhythms.

Example 0a

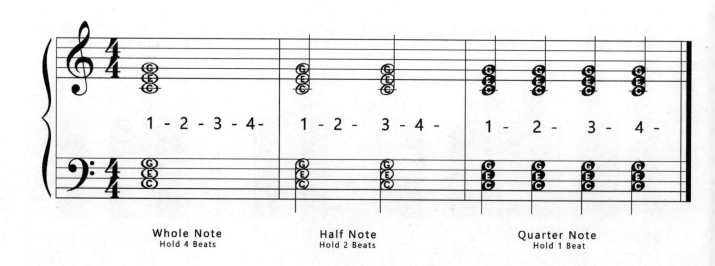

Chapter One: Major Chords

The notes we play affect the sound and feeling of the music, and a chord is a collection of three or more notes played at the same time.

The first set of chords you need to learn on the piano are *Major* chords. These chords form the backbone of most pop and rock songs and are an essential part of all music. By learning these major chords you won't only begin to develop a palette of sounds you can use to play songs, you will start to learn how your hand should move between chords on the piano.

All major chords follow the same patterns, and those patterns are easy to find.

Let's learn to play the chord of C Major.

Start by placing your right thumb on the note C and letting each finger rest on an adjacent piano key. Don't skip any keys or any fingers while you're finding your position. If you have trouble remembering where the keys are, or which finger is which, use the reference page at the beginning of this book until you have these memorized. Once each finger is resting on a note, finger 5 (your pinkie) should be on the note G.

To play the C Major chord, lift fingers 2 and 4 slightly so they are not touching the keys. Keep your wrist straight and lower your arm so that fingers 1, 3 and 5 press into the keys. Use the weight of your arm to play the chord rather than pushing down each individual finger.

Example 1a:

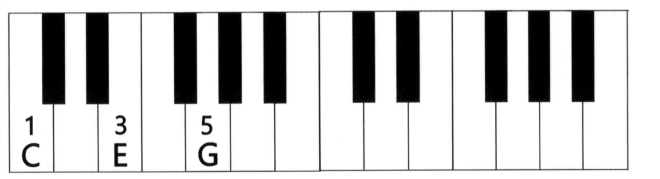

The next figure shows how the C Major chord looks when notated on the staff. The lowest note is played on *middle C* – the C nearest the middle of the piano. Find this note on your keyboard and play a C Major chord with your right hand.

The next notated chord starts on *treble C*, which is next the C to the right of middle C. Find treble C and play a C Major chord with your right hand.

Then find the next C to the right and play another C Major chord with your right hand. Keep going until you reach the end of the keyboard.

Example 1b:

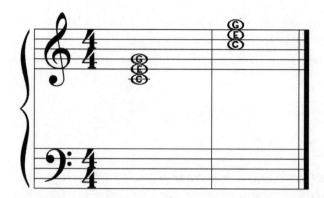

Let's use this same fingering pattern to build another chord: G Major.

Move your right thumb to the note G above middle C and let each finger rest on an adjacent key. Once again, fingers 1, 3 and 5 will play, while fingers 2 and 4 do not.

When you find the G Major chord, play it a few times to familiarize your hand with the feel of the chord. Then, move up the keyboard, find another G, and build the chord again. Repeat this process until you reach the end of the keyboard.

Example 1c:

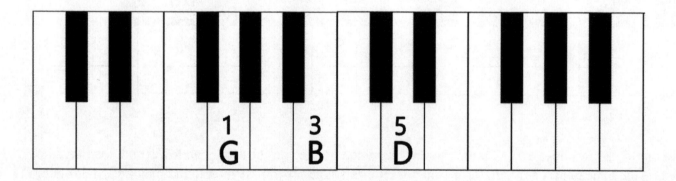

Now let's play F Major. Place your thumb on the note F and repeat the process to find the F Major chord. Notice that it's very close to the G Major chord. The notes have simply shifted one key to the left. Play the F Major chord a few times, then work your way up the keyboard, finding each F and building an F Major chord on it until you reach the end of the keyboard.

Example 1d:

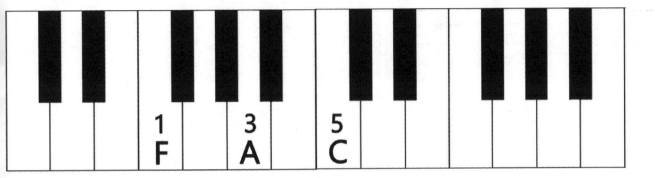

Congratulations! You're playing chords on the piano and making music! Repeat this lesson as often as you like to practice building major chords with your right hand.

Now let's play the same chords with your left hand. The notes of the chord remain the same no matter which hand is playing, but because your hands are shaped differently, you will use different fingers for each note.

Place finger 5 of the left hand on bass C – the C below middle C. Rest each finger rest on a key so that finger 1 (your thumb) ends up on G. Once again, slightly raise fingers 2 and 4 and lower your arm to play the notes of the chord.

Example 1e:

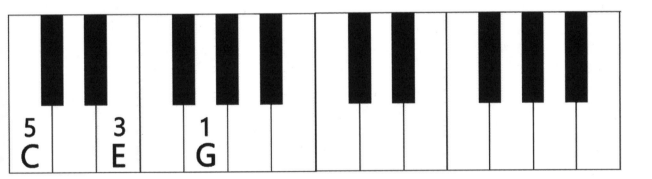

Play the C Major chord with your left hand a few times, then find the C to the left of bass C and build a C Major chord on that note. The following example shows what this movement looks like when written on the staff.

Example 1f:

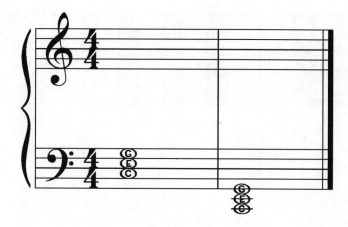

Once you have found the C Major chord below bass C, continue to move to the left and build C Major chords until you reach the end of the keyboard.

Now let's build a G Major chord with your left hand. As with C Major, the notes in the G Major chord are the same no matter which hand you play it with.

Example 1g:

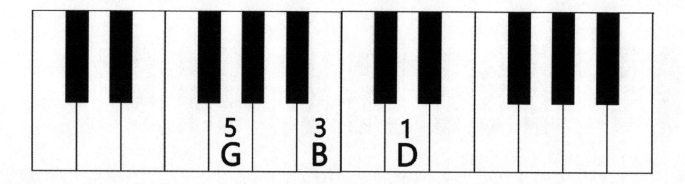

Once you have found G Major, play it a few times before locating the G to the left and moving there to build a new chord. Work your way down the piano, playing G Major chords until you reach the end of the keyboard.

When you have completed that, return to the center of the piano and build an F Major chord. Once again, it'll be just one note lower than the G Major chord.

Example 1h:

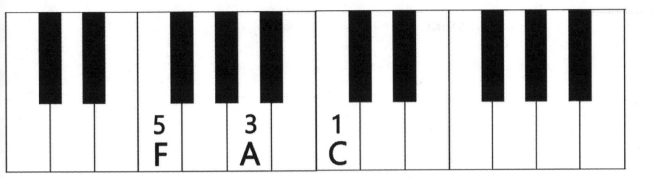

Play the F Major chord several times, then work your way down the piano, building F Major chords until you reach the end of the keyboard.

Congratulations! You're ready to start playing songs!

Playing Songs with Major Chords

Most songs contain multiple chords, so you must learn to switch quickly from one chord to another. Chords often repeat the same pattern throughout a song to create a *progression*. Learning progressions will enable you to easily play any song and write your own songs using that chord progression.

Let's start with a two-chord progression: C Major to G Major.

Play the C Major chord with your right hand. Notice that the note G is played with finger 5. Being aware of the G note's position on the keyboard will make it easier to move to the G Major chord.

Example 1i:

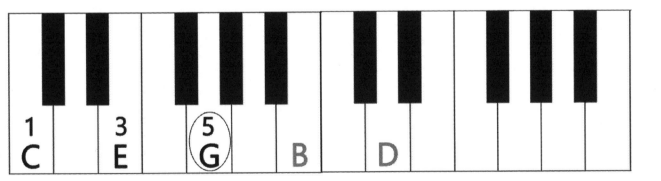

Lift your hand off the keyboard and move to the G chord. The note that was played by finger 5 is now played by finger 1. Resist the temptation to slide along the keys and instead lift your whole arm in an arching motion as you make the move. This builds muscle memory faster and helps you move more efficiently. I call this technique "lift and land" and it's vital to playing chords well.

Now use the same lifting motion to move back to the C chord. Finger 1 will settle on the note C and finger 5 will return to the G. Practice moving back and forth between these two chords. Focus on the lift and land technique as you practice this progression.

Now let's play this progression with the left hand. It can be tempting to skip training both hands, especially if one hand is slower than the other, but you will need to play with both hands to become an accomplished pianist. If one hand is weaker, give it a little extra practice to help it catch up.

Notice that the finger pattern is reversed in the left hand. Finger 1 plays the note G, and you will move finger 5 to it.

Example 1j:

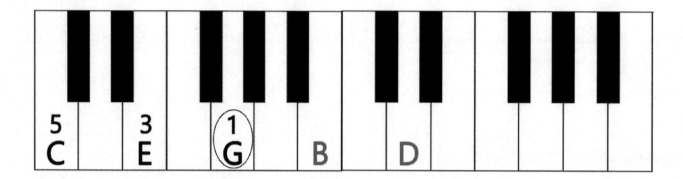

Practice this progression with the left hand, moving between the chords as you learn to lift your hand off the keys and land in the correct position. If you have trouble finding the correct notes as you move, being aware of the black keys can help. The note C is located to the left of the group of two black keys. G is located inside a group of three black keys. These groups are useful landmarks for navigating the keyboard.

Congratulations! You have learned your first chord progression! Let's put it into a song.

Lead sheets are a type of music notation that show you which chords to play. They are a great way to quickly learn a song. I read sheet music well, but I still love using lead sheets because of their streamlined simplicity.

You may have noticed that each chord you have learned so far is named after its first note. The chord that starts on C is called C Major. The chord that starts on G is called G Major. This is true for every chord you will learn. The technical term for that first note is the *root*, and chords are always named after their root.

* * *

In the next exercise, you will play the C Major to G Major chord progression along with an audio track to practice quick movements between chords. Each chord will last for four beats, but you must lift earlier than that to allow yourself time to change between chords. Your goal is to hold down the chord to sustain the sound for as long as possible, but lift early enough to give yourself time to move to the new chord and play it at the right time.

Before you play this song, listen to the audio and tap along to familiarize yourself with the beat and the music. The notated example repeats and you will play it twice for a total of eight chords. Playing with an audio track is a great way to master switching chords. You must coordinate your movements with the music so you land on each chord at exactly the right moment. It takes practice to coordinate these movements and perform them with perfect rhythm.

Have fun and don't worry if it takes a while to get the timing just right.

Example 1k:

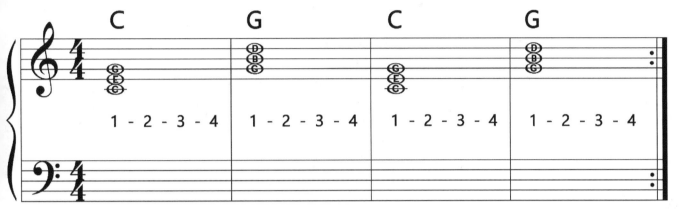

Now, play along with the audio but instead of playing the entire chords, only play the notes C and G with your thumb. As you build muscle memory and are able to move more quickly between chords, you will need less time to make the move. Listen to the rhythm of the music to help your timing.

When you can move from the single notes C and G in time with the music, repeat the exercise playing all three notes of the chords. Let your thumb lead as you lift and land from chord to chord. If you can land finger 1 on the correct note, the rest of your hand will follow.

It's okay to hit some wrong notes while you learn this exercise. If you still can't play the correct chords in time after some practice, go back to the beginning of this chapter and review the chords again. I often have my students practice individual chords for several weeks before we move on to chord progressions.

Now let's play the same song with the left hand!

Example 1l:

First practice moving between chords by playing just the notes C and G with finger 5 of your left hand. Play along with the audio and focus on using good lift and land technique to build muscle memory in your left hand. Keep finger 5 curved rather than flat, as that gives you more strength and control.

When you're comfortable playing the single notes, repeat the exercise using the full chords. Lift off the chord as early as you need to arrive at the next chord on time. Speed and security will come with practice.

If you notice that one hand or chord is weaker than the other as you're playing this song, give it some extra practice and a chance to catch up.

Once you can play this song easily, have fun with it! You can find these chords in many places on your instrument so experiment with playing the chords in the low, middle and high ranges of the keyboard. The piano sounds different in its high and low registers, so you can get a lot of different tones with just these two chords.

* * *

The next progression uses all three of the chords you have learned in this order:

C Major, F Major, G Major, F Major.

Moving from F Major to G Major is easy, as you only have to move your hand over one key. You practiced moving from G Major to C Major in the last exercise, so the only new movement in this progression is from C Major to F Major.

Practice that move slowly and pay attention to the location of each root note. Remember to lift off the keys as you move and use the root of your chord as a guide to find the new chord.

Listen to the audio and tap along with the beat. Counting out loud is a great way to develop your sense of rhythm.

Once you're familiar with the music, play this example using only the roots of the chords. Play each root with your right thumb as you lift and land to move from chord to chord. When you can do that in time with the audio, add the rest of the notes to play the full chords.

Example 1m:

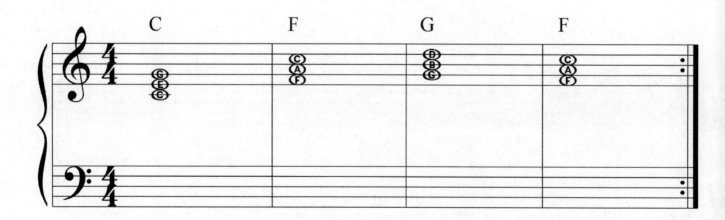

Now play that progression with the left hand.

Example 1n:

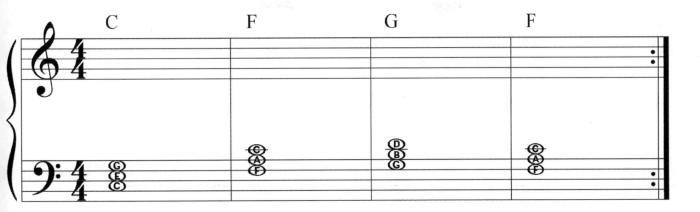

Practice playing just the roots notes first, each with finger 5 of the left hand. Lift and land between the chords, building muscle memory until you can easily make the movement between the chords in time with the audio. Then add the other notes of the chords. Let finger 5 lead as the rest of your hand falls into place.

Try exploring this major chord shape starting on different notes to see what sounds they make.

Now you've discovered the sound of major chords, let's change the mood and move on to learning how to play and move between *minor* chords.

Chapter Two: Minor Chords

In Chapter One, you learned how to play C Major, F Major and G Major chords. Now you will learn three *minor* chords. The terms major and minor refer to the chord *quality* – a term that describes the chord's sound. Generally, major chords sound happy and bright, while minor chords sound sad and dark. Music is almost always formed from combinations of these characteristics.

Let's learn to play D minor.

Place your right thumb on the note D. Let each finger rest on an adjacent key and play fingers 1, 3 and 5. Repeat the chord a few times and listen to the sound of D minor.

Example 2a:

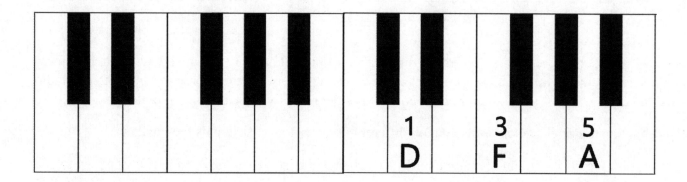

Now play the D minor chord with your left hand. Remember to place finger 5 (pinkie) on the lowest root note and then build the chord.

Example 2b:

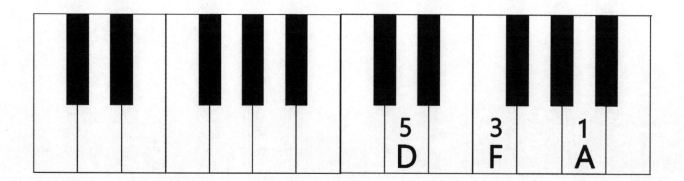

Let's listen the difference in sound between major and minor chords.

With your right hand, play the C Major chord a few times and listen to the sound. Then move to D minor and play that chord several times. Do you hear a difference? Minor chords are often said to sound sad or dramatic, while major chords sound happy and cheerful. Some people hear this difference right away, while others develop their ability to hear differences in chord quality over time. As long as you keep playing and listening, your ability to distinguish between different types of chords will continue to improve.

Let's learn another minor chord. Move your right thumb to the note E and follow the process you have learned to find the E minor chord. Move up the keyboard and play an E minor chord high on the piano. Then move down the keyboard and play the chord low on the piano. Lead with your thumb as you lift and land.

Example 2c:

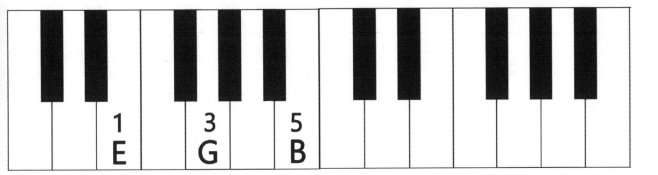

Now play E Minor with the left hand. Lead with finger 5 as you find the root and the notes for the chord. Play it high and low on the keyboard as you practice finding the note E with finger 5 and landing on the chord.

Example 2d:

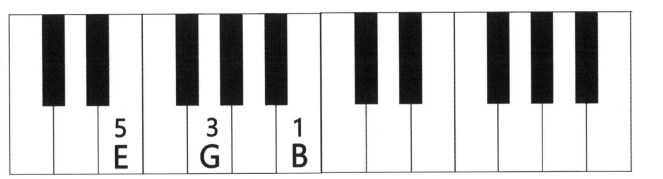

For the final minor chord in this chapter, challenge yourself by finding it with your left hand first. Find the note A with finger 5, then follow the process you have learned to discover the rest of the notes. Then find the lowest A on the piano and use it to build an A minor chord. Play the chord, hold it down, and listen to the sound until it fades away.

Example 2e:

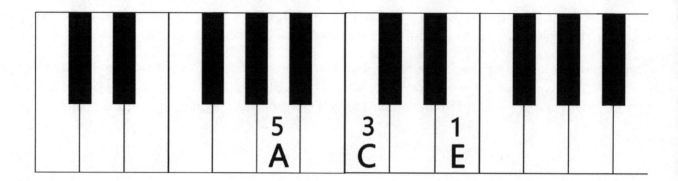

Next, play the A minor chord with your right hand. Then find the highest note A on your piano, play an A minor chord, and listen to the sound as it fades away. Notice how the high sounds on the piano fade more quickly than the low sounds. This is useful to know when you start writing your own songs or creating arrangements.

Example 2f:

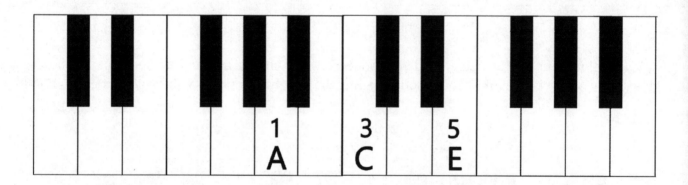

Review the minor chords as often as needed until you can find and play them quickly with both hands.

In time, you will know these chords so well that you can play them easily without thinking, but it takes practice to develop that skill. Enjoy the journey as you expand your musical abilities.

Playing Songs with Minor Chords

Most songs use a mixture of major and minor chords. This means that musicians need a way to differentiate between the two.

In lead sheets, minor chords are shown by including a lowercase letter "m" after the root of the chord. So the D minor chord is labeled "Dm". As you saw in Chapter One, major chords are notated by showing the chord root with no additional symbols. Look at the notation and lead sheet in Example 2g. The second chord is an A minor chord. The lowercase "m" in the lead sheet shows that the chord is minor.

Example 2g:

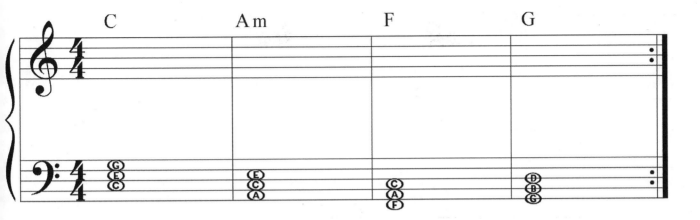

Now that you know how to read a lead sheet with major and minor chords, you're ready to learn some more songs and progressions. Listen to Example 2h and tap along with the beat to hear where the chords change before playing the root note of each chord with finger 1. Count to four as you hold each note before changing.

Example 2h:

When you can comfortably play the roots of the chords in time, add the other notes and play the entire chord. After you have played this exercise in the middle of the piano as written, find these chords higher and lower on the keyboard and repeat the exercise.

Repeat this exercise as many times as you like and feel free to come back to it for extra practice.

Example 2i shows the same song notated for your left hand. First practice playing the chord roots with finger 5, then add the other notes to build the full chords.

Example 2i:

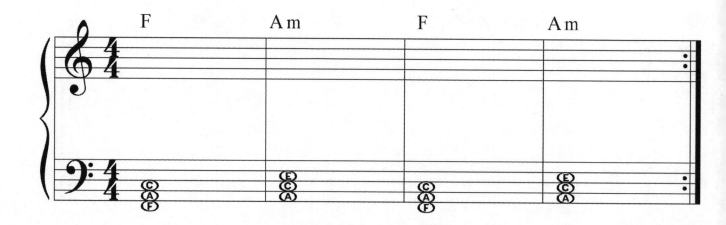

Once you can play this example along with the audio with your left hand, move down the keyboard to find these chords lower on the piano and play it again.

Let's play a song that uses both hands for the first time. Practice slowly without the audio first to develop this new skill. Make sure you can find the C Major chord with both hands before you begin so that you don't have to pause mid-song to place your left hand in measure three. Play this exercise several times without worrying about rhythm, taking as long as you need to coordinate the hands.

Example 2j:

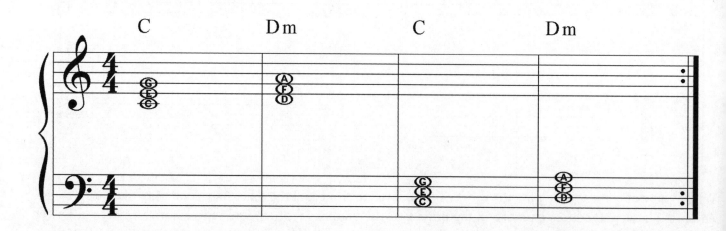

When you can comfortably move both hands at a slow pace, start counting four beats for each chord to practice moving in time. Use the four beats of each chord to think ahead and prepare for the next chord. When you can play this example with slow counts, play along with the audio.

Have patience as you learn to play with both hands. Many of my students find playing with both hands to be the most difficult part of playing the piano, but it becomes easier and easier the more you practice.

Let's go back to playing with one hand and learn a longer progression with major and minor chords. This time, you will learn the progression with your left hand first.

Example 2k:

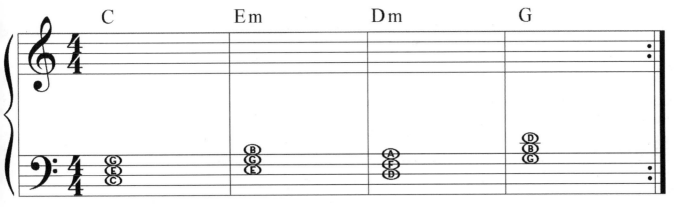

Listen to the audio. Count out loud and tap along to familiarize yourself with the beat. Practice first with the roots played by finger 5, then add the full chords when you're confident. Focus on lifting and landing cleanly on each chord without sliding from side to side along the keys to search for it.

Now learn the song with your right hand, playing the roots with your thumb first, then adding the rest of the notes.

Relax and have fun as you travel from chord to chord. You're making music!

Example 2l:

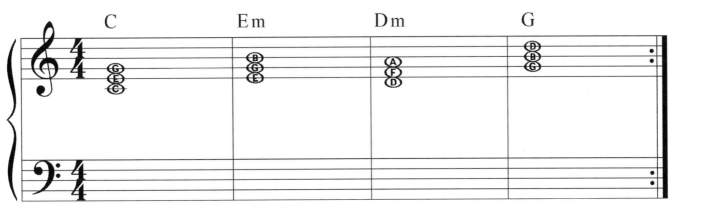

Chapter Three: Songs in C Major

In music, a *key* is a collection of notes and chords that go together. Just as chords are named by their roots, keys are named after their first note and the quality of their first chord. The key based on the note C is called C Major.

In this chapter, you will learn three of the most popular pop chord progressions in the key of C Major. The six chords you have learned so far can be used to play lots of music in the key of C Major. It is a popular key for piano music because it uses only the white notes on the piano!

We often use Roman numerals to label chord progressions, and I will do that in this book so you can recognize these progressions in the future.

The first chord in the key (C Major) is called "chord one", the second (D minor) is called "chord two" etc, all the way to chord seven. We use Roman numerals instead of the number so we don't get confused with all the other things we number when playing music (fingers, notes, distances, bars and beats).

With the Roman numeral system, the chords are given the following labels:

C Major (chord one) = I

F Major (chord four) = IV

G Major (chord five) = V

A minor (chord six) = vi (notice that minor chords use lowercase Roman numerals)

To calculate the position of a chord in a key, simply count up the scale from the root note.

Chord	1 / I	2 / ii	3 / iii	4 / IV	5 / V	6 / vi	7 / vii°
Note	C	D	E	F	G	A	B

A chord progression is a repeating sequence of chords that repeat throughout the whole song. If these progressions sound familiar, there's a good reason for that. They have been used in songs for centuries, and you have likely heard them before.

Once you know how to play a progression, you can use it to play any song that uses that sequence – there are actually far fewer common chord progressions than you might think!

Progression One: I – vi – IV – V

Example 3a shows a popular four-chord progression that's sometimes called the '*50s progression* because it was very popular in the doo-wop music of the 1950s. You may recognize it from songs like *Heart and Soul* or *Stand by Me,* but it was used before then by classical composers like Bach and Mozart, and continues to be popular with musicians today. More modern songs that use this progression include *Million Reasons* (Lady Gaga), *Perfect* (Ed Sheeran) and *This is Me* (The Greatest Showman soundtrack).

Listen to the audio for Example 3a, then play along using your right hand. Have fun and feel the beat as you make music!

Example 3a:

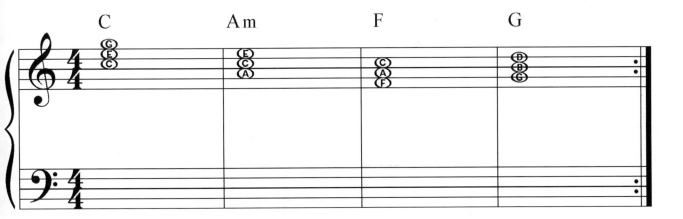

Example 3b uses the same progression with a different musical style. Listen to the audio first and tap along to feel the new beat. Then play the progression with your left hand.

Example 3b:

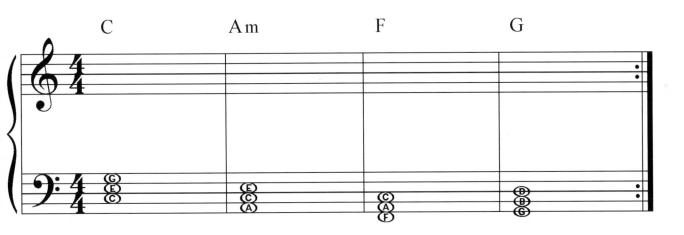

Progression Two: I – V – vi – IV

This next progression uses the same four chords in a different order. It's also very popular in music across a variety of genres and can be heard in such songs as *Take Me Home, Country Roads* (John Denver), *Any Way You Want It* (Journey) and *Demons* (Imagine Dragons).

Play the two examples below one hand at a time. Notice how reordering these chords changes the sound of the progression. You can create a lot of different songs with just a few chords!

Example 3c:

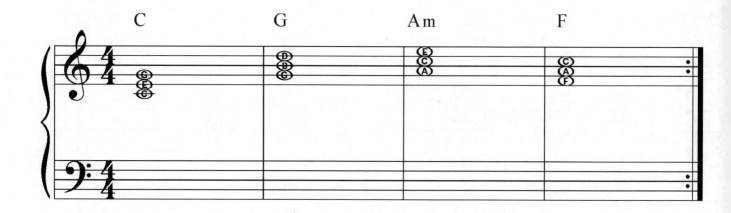

Now let's play this progression with the left hand and a different musical style. Listen to the audio for Example 3d and tap along with the beat, then play the progression with the audio. Relax and feel the beat.

Example 3d:

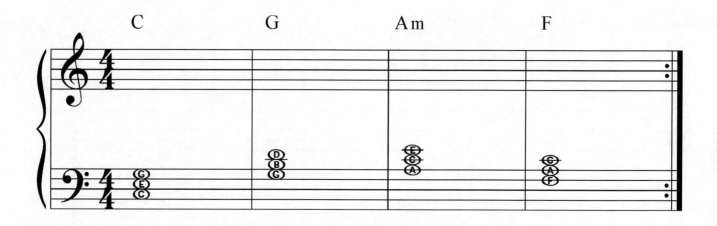

Progression Three: vi – IV – I – V

The next progression is another variation on the same four chords. This time you start with the A minor chord which adds a melancholy feel to the music. This progression can be heard in songs such as *What About Love* (Heart), *Despacito* (Luis Fonsi ft. Daddy Yankee) and *All of Me* (John Legend).

Even though this progression uses the same four chords as the others, it will still take some practice to move easily between them when they're in a different order. Let's practice this progression.

Example 3e:

Listen to the audio to establish the beat, then play along. Count to four while holding each chord and think ahead so you're ready to lift and land. Counting in your head or out loud is a great way to keep track of the beat as you play. Even very experienced musicians use counting to stay on track as they play.

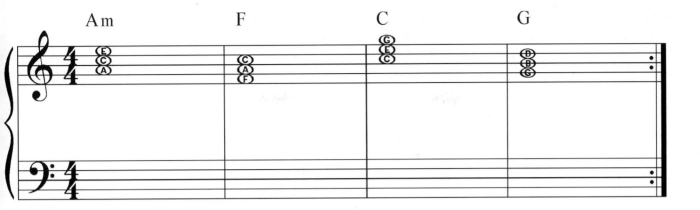

Example 3f:

This example uses the same chord progression in a difference style. Listen to the audio to establish the beat, then play along with your left hand.

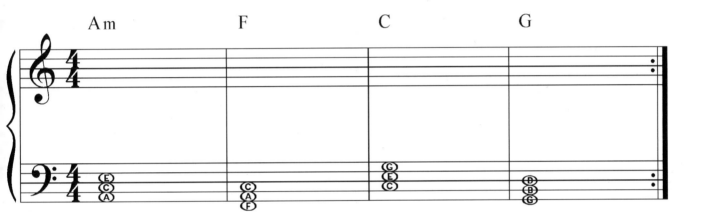

If you have trouble keeping in time with any of the examples in this book, simplify them by playing with only the root note. Once you can play the example easily with a single note, add the rest of the chord. The practice techniques you learn in each chapter are all tools that can help you master new progressions and songs down the road. Don't be afraid to take a step back and use different approaches if you have trouble mastering a song.

These three progressions will allow you to play thousands of songs in many genres. With experience, you'll quickly be able to identify a song's chord progression by ear and this will help you learn it more quickly. Look for patterns and repetitions every time you learn a new song. It'll save you a lot of time and make you a stronger musician.

Now let's put these progressions into practice with longer songs.

Practice Exercises

Example 3g uses the I – vi – IV – V progression. You will play the progression four times (including the repeat), alternating between your right hand and left hand.

Place both hands on C Major chords before you begin so that the left hand is ready to play. Use the four beats to think ahead to the next chord so you're prepared to move and switch hands.

Example 3g:

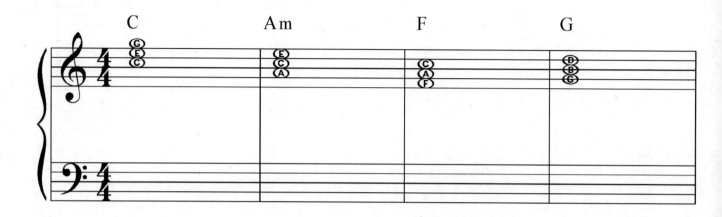

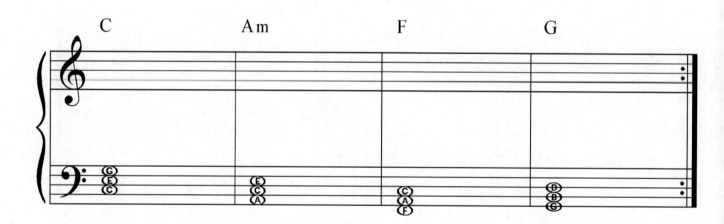

Now let's play through the I – V – vi – IV progression with an upbeat tempo. This time, you will start with your left hand, then continue with your right. Practice this example slowly without the track first, paying close attention to the places where you transition between the hands. Think ahead and lift the hands early if needed so you can play the next chord on time.

Coordinating chord changes and hand switches can be tricky, so take things slowly until you feel comfortable with the progression. Then play along with the audio and have fun rocking out with this popular progression.

Example 3h:

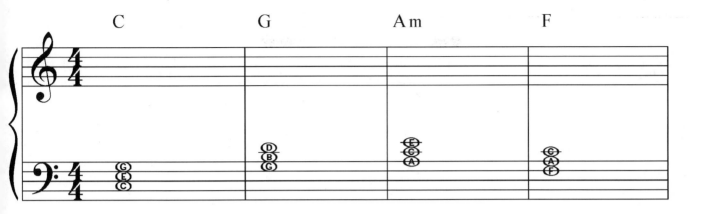

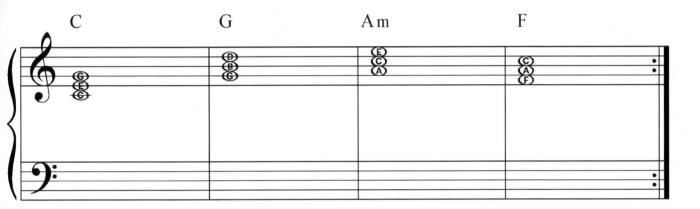

Play the following example, which uses the vi – IV – I – V progression. Place both hands on the A minor chord before you begin and use the time you're holding the chords to think ahead to what comes next. Play this progression without the audio first so you can go slowly and practice the moves. Then play along with the audio.

Example 3i:

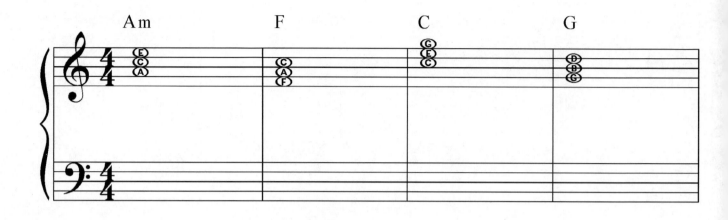

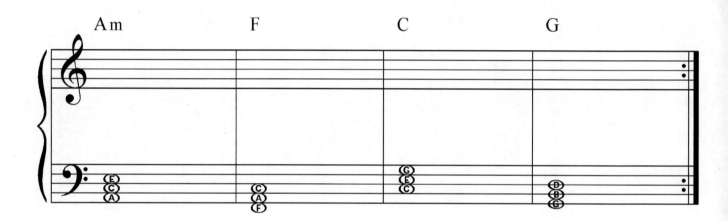

Let's use what you've learned to create your own music. Write your own four-chord progression using any of the chords you have learned so far in whatever order you like. Play the chords and feel free to experiment until you find an order you like. Then create a lead sheet by writing down the chord names in order.

Play your progression, holding each chord for four beats and repeat the progression several times with each hand. If you want a different sound, play your progression high or low on the piano. Experiment until you find a sound that suits your progression and the musical effect you want to create.

Congratulations! You have learned several songs on the piano and written your own.

Chapter Four: Basic Accompaniment Patterns

As you listen to music, you'll notice that pianists often vary the way in which they play their chords. They repeat chords, split them up, and change rhythms to make the music more interesting. You're ready to do the same!

These different ways to change chords are called *accompaniment patterns.* Like chord progressions, accompaniment patterns often repeat throughout a song. Once you learn how to play an accompaniment pattern, you can apply it to *any* chord progression or song that you learn in the future.

Let's get started!

Block Chords

So far, you have been playing *block chords,* which are simply chords with all the notes played at the same time. There are many ways to vary block chords to add interest to your music.

Let's start by repeating these chords on each beat. Since the sound of the piano fades away quickly after you play it, this is a great way to make the sound last longer and adds a rhythmic drive to your playing. Songs that use repeated block chord accompaniment patterns include *When I Was Your Man* (Bruno Mars), *I Look to You* (Whitney Houston) and *Let It Be* (Beatles). While this pattern is often used in ballads, songs like *Brave* (Sara Bareilles) use this accompaniment pattern to create a lot of energy.

To repeat a chord, lift your arm straight up then drop back into the keys. Hold the shape of the chord in the air so your fingers play the same notes as you come down. The motion comes from your arm. It's difficult to play repeated chords with your fingers, but very easy if you use the lift and land technique and let your arm do the work.

Example 4a uses the C Major chord with a repeating block chord accompaniment pattern. Notice that the example only contains one lead sheet symbol at the very beginning, even though many chords are played. This is because all these chords have the same root, so it's not necessary to include additional lead sheet symbols. This is standard practice in lead sheet notation: you continue to play the same chord until you see another symbol.

Example 4a:

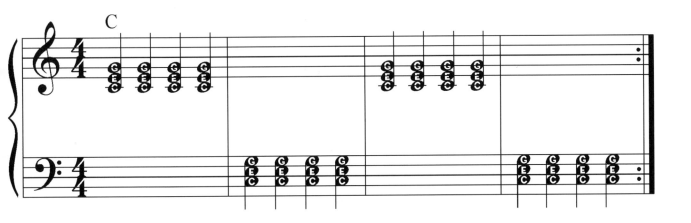

Feel free to tap your foot, nod your head, or sway along with the music. These things can help you keep your beat and stay loose and relaxed as you play.

Now let's play an example using this accompaniment pattern with changing chords. Use the lifting motion in your arm to help you move quickly to your next chord. As with previous examples, use the root as a guide as you move.

Example 4b:

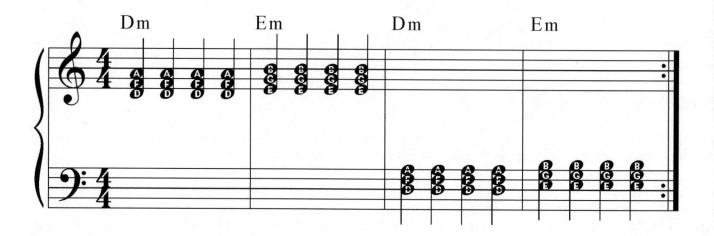

As you repeat the chords, look and think ahead to prepare for changes. Playing with both hands requires a lot of concentration, so it helps to be mentally prepared and get both hands in the correct place on the keyboard before you begin.

Not all block chord accompaniment patterns use the same rhythm. Let's try an example with a changing rhythm. Example 4c includes the counts in the sheet music to help you keep track of the beat. Hold the first chord for two beats, then play again on beats 3 and 4 of the bar.

Play along with the audio and count the rhythm out loud as you play. Settle into the groove and think of yourself as a drummer as you repeat the chords by lifting your arm. The piano is often used as a percussion part to keep the beat in songs.

Example 4c:

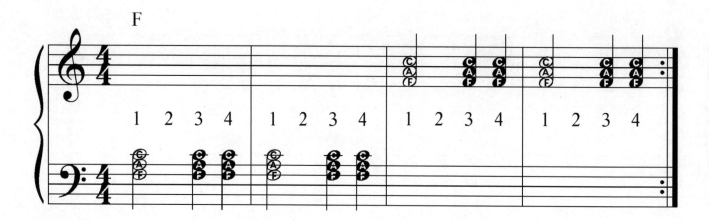

For further practice, try adding block chord accompaniment patterns with all the chord progressions we've covered so far. You can also apply it to the progression you wrote in Chapter Three.

Broken Chords

Broken chords are another popular accompaniment pattern. As the name suggests, this accompaniment pattern breaks chords apart into individual notes. You can hear this pattern in songs like *Someone Like You* (Adele), *Fallin'* (Alicia Keys) and *Clocks* (Coldplay).

While you play repeated block chords by lifting your arms, you play broken chords with your fingers and you don't need to lift your arm until you change chords. Use the same fingers to play the broken chord that you would use to play the block chord.

Play Example 4d on your own, before playing it along with the audio. While you don't need to lift your arm to play broken chords, you may rock or rotate slightly at the wrist to make this motion easier. Keep your hands, arms and shoulders loose as the fingers play individually. Stiffness adds tension and hinders your playing. As pianists, our goal is always to stay loose and relaxed as we play.

Example 4d:

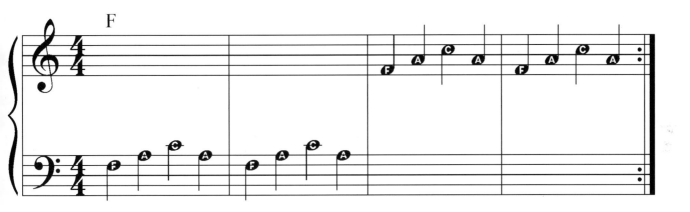

The notes of a broken chord can be played in any order, which gives you many options for creating different sounds. The accompaniment pattern in Example 4e is sometimes called the Alberti bass pattern. It was a particular favorite of classical composers like Mozart and Beethoven and continues to be popular today.

Example 4e:

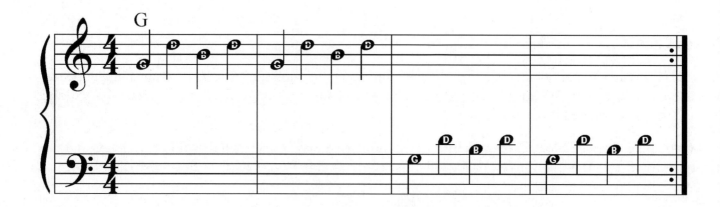

Keep your arm loose and allow your hand to rock from side to side as you play. Once you've got the idea, move your hands higher on the keyboard and play the example again, noticing the difference in sound. Move your hands lower on the keyboard and play it once more.

Now let's practice playing broken patterns while changing chords. Use the same lift and land motion to move between the broken chords that you would for block chords. Focus on finding and playing the root first and letting the rest of your fingers fall into place. Lead with finger 1 in the right hand and finger 5 in the left hand.

As you play the pattern, think ahead to your next chord just as you did when playing block chords in Chapter Three. This will take some practice, but eventually you will build muscle memory and be able to play the broken chords without having to focus much attention on them.

Example 4f:

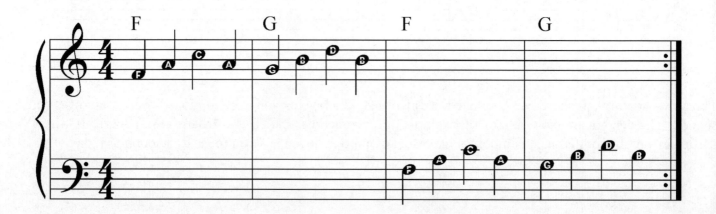

Congratulations! You have taken your playing to the next level with accompaniment patterns. Let's apply your new skills to playing longer songs.

Practice Exercises

This song uses the I – vi – IV – V progression that you learned in Chapter Three with a repeated block chord accompaniment pattern.

When it's time to change chords, use the lifting motion as the beginning of a lift and land, and find the root of the next chord. Think ahead so you're prepared for each move.

This accompaniment pattern is percussive in nature, so let your played notes as well as your lifting motions settle into a groove that works with the music.

Example 4g:

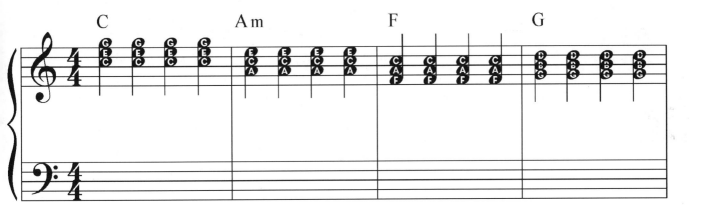

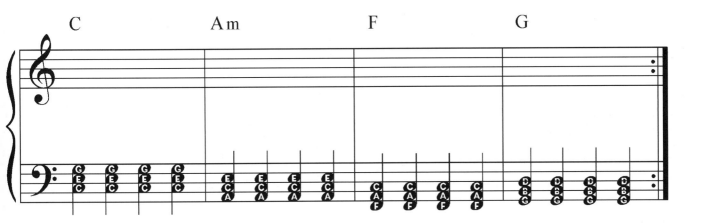

The next example uses the I – V – vi – IV progression with a broken chord accompaniment pattern. Notice how moving between broken chords feels different from moving between block chords. In some ways, broken chord movements are easier because you only have to play the root of the chord at first. You have a little extra time to find the rest of the notes as you play, although you still want to settle all your fingers on the keys as soon as you can.

It'll take time and practice to develop this coordination, so have patience and remember to have fun while playing. If you get frustrated with any of these exercises, try playing them without the audio at a slower tempo to give your hands a chance to build muscle memory for the new pattern.

Example 4h:

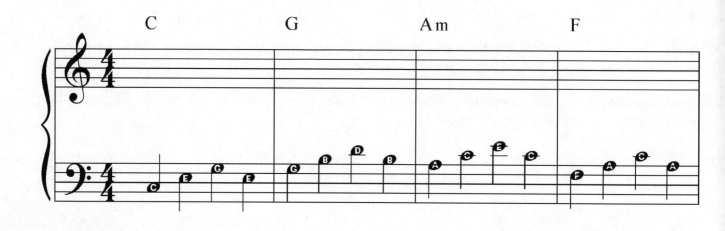

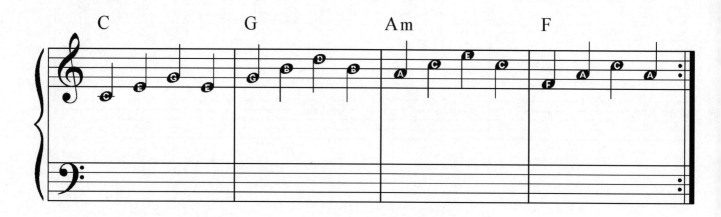

The next song uses the vi – IV – I – V progression with a slower blocked accompaniment pattern. Each chord holds for two beats, but you can lift early to change chords. One of the tricky things about playing slow accompaniment patterns is keeping track of the beat. It's just as easy to rush ahead and play chords too soon as it is to lag behind and play them too late. Do your best to count, listen and stay right with the beat as you play.

Feel free to sway, nod your head, or tap your foot along with the beat to help you feel the rhythm of the music. Personally, I love playing ballads because the slower tempo gives me more time to enjoy the music.

Example 4i:

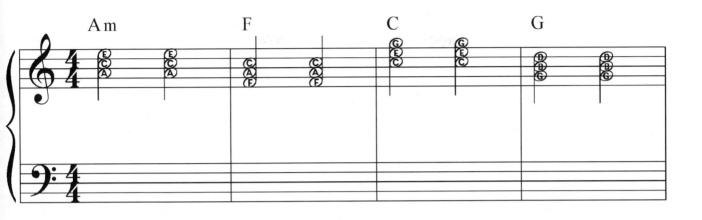

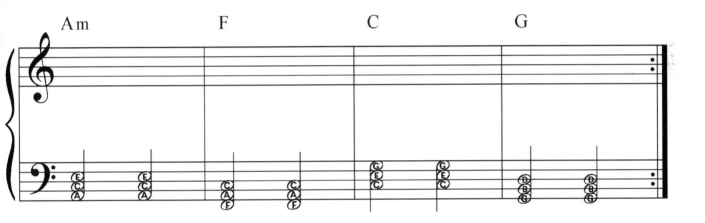

Now that you've played a variety of accompaniment patterns, you're ready to create your own. Play the progression notated in Example 4j. When you can move easily between the chords, choose one of the block chord accompaniment patterns you learned in this chapter and apply it to the progression. Play the progression with the accompaniment pattern several times, until it feels easy and natural to play the chords with that rhythm.

Example 4j:

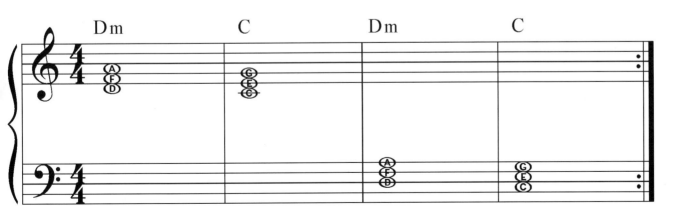

Here are a few examples of different ways to vary the progression with accompaniment patterns. Feel free to play through these for inspiration as you experiment with your own ideas.

Figure 4a:

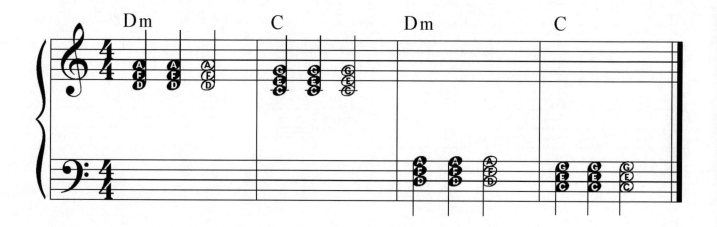

Figure 4b:

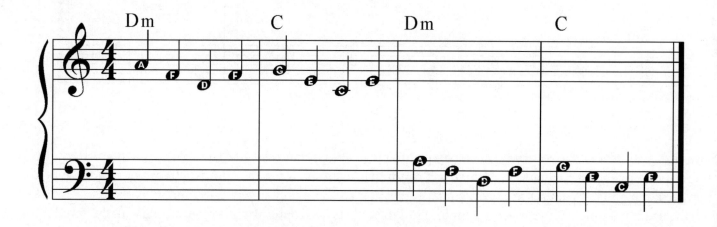

Keep things simple as you practice accompaniment patterns. Have fun trying different rhythms and combinations as you make your own music. Once you find a pattern you like, repeat it a few times to create a song. For more variety, try moving to different places on the piano or combining chord progressions by playing four bars of one then four bars of another. Have fun as you create your own unique songs.

Chapter Five: Chord Inversions

So far, you have played chords in *root position,* where each chord's root is played in the bass as the lowest note of the chord. This is an easy way to identify what chord you're playing and learn the notes of each one, but it can be difficult to jump from chord to chord when playing quickly or using accompaniment patterns. Playing every chord in root position also doesn't give you a very smooth sound. Playing chords in *inversions* eliminates those problems and gives you even more ways to play chords on the piano.

An *inverted* chord is simply one where the note order is rearranged. Example 5a shows the C Major chord in different inversions. No matter what order they are in, the notes C, E and G create a C Major chord.

Moving the note C from the bottom to the top of the chord creates a *first inversion* chord. Repeating that process and moving the note E from the bottom to the top creates a *second inversion* chord.

Example 5a

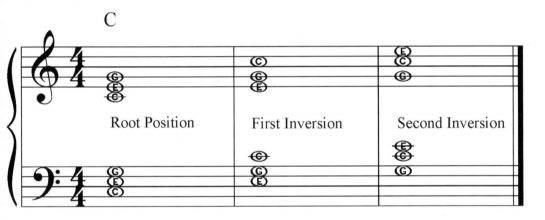

I often have my students practice root position chords for several weeks before teaching them inversions, so go back and review Chapter One and Chapter Two if you get lost or confused at any point. The better you know the notes in each major and minor chord, the easier it is to play inversions.

Playing Technique for Chord Inversions

When you invert a chord, the notes are no longer spaced evenly with a single skipped white key between each one. An inversion will always create a wider gap between two notes which means that you must use different fingerings and stretch your hand slightly to reach the keys. The right hand plays first inversion chords with fingers 1, 2 and 5.

Spread your fingers slightly so you can reach the notes. Unless you have a very small hand, this should be an easy reach. It will take some practice to get used to playing with finger 2 and an expanded hand position, but it shouldn't create strain or tension. Play this chord a few times as you notice how it feels and sounds. Then move up the piano and play the same chord on higher notes. Remember to bring the arm down to play the chord rather than playing with the individual fingers.

Example 5b:

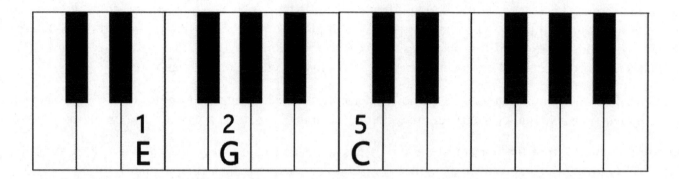

The right hand plays second inversion chords with fingers 1, 3 and 5. Your thumb has the most reach out of your fingers, so let it stretch down as you play this chord. Play the notes below and repeat the chord a few times as you get used to the different feeling and sound. Move up the piano and play the chord on higher notes.

Example 5c:

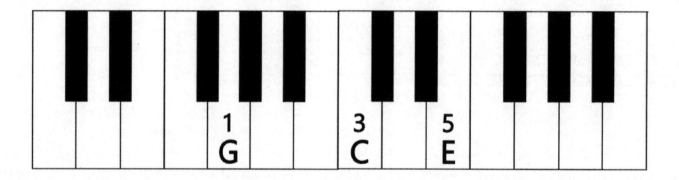

Now let's practice inversions with the left hand. Example 5d shows a first inversion C Major chord with left hand fingering. Play it a few times to get used to the feel and sound. Then move lower on the piano and play this chord on the lower notes.

Example 5d:

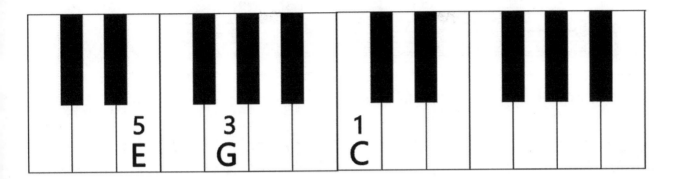

When you have played the first inversion C Major chord with your left hand a few times, use Example 5e to find the second inversion. The left hand will play second inversion chords with fingers 1, 2 and 5. As you did with the right hand, spread your fingers slightly to help you reach the notes. It should be an easy reach and not create tension in the hand.

Play the second inversion chord with your left hand a few times to get used to the different feeling and sound. Then move down the keyboard and play it again on lower notes.

Example 5e:

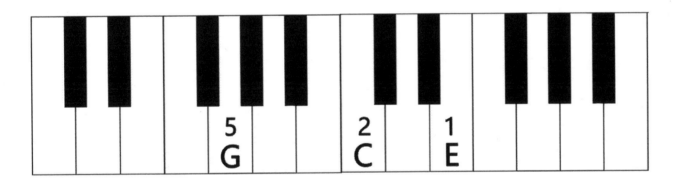

Now let's play more chord inversions. Pay careful attention to your fingering. Remember that the right hand plays first inversion chords with fingers 1, 2 and 5, while the left hand uses that fingering for second inversion chords.

Example 5f shows inversions for the G Major chord. Play the root position chord with your right hand first, then find and play the first and second inversions. When you can comfortably play the chords with your right hand, play them with your left. Each inversion should contain the notes G, B, and D in a different order.

Example 5f:

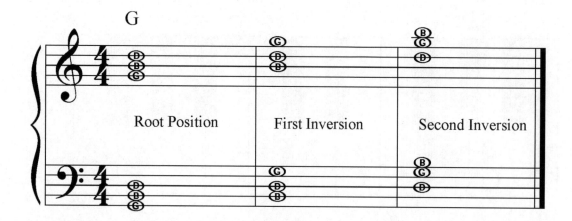

Take your time as you learn to play these inversions. If something sounds strange, trust your ear and double check that you're playing the notes G, B and D. Remember to use the lift and land motion for ease of playing as you move between chords.

Let's repeat this process with the F Major chord. For a challenge, start with your left hand this time. Use Example 5g as your guide and make sure that each inversion contains the notes F, A and C. Make sure you use the correct fingering for each chord. If you find yourself confused about the fingering, refer back to Examples 5b-5e for help.

Example 5g:

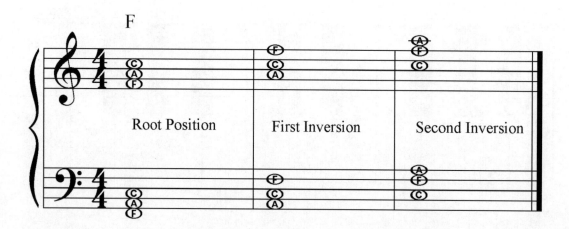

Congratulations! You are ready to take the next step with chord inversions.

Progressions with Chord Inversions

You did a lot of work in the previous section but the good news is that you're ready to use chord inversions in songs. When you only use root position chords, moving between chords often results in large hand movements. Using inversions allows you to move easily between chords and create a much smoother sound or better *voice leading*.

Here is the very first progression you learned: C Major to G Major. Play the following exercise to review what it feels like to play it using root position chords. Notice how far you have to move your hand and how the transition does not sound smooth.

Example 5h:

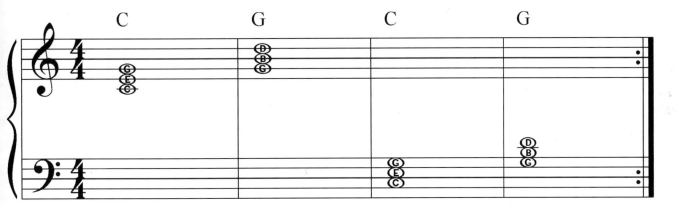

Now let's play this progression using inversions.

By using a first inversion G Major chord you can keep your hand in the same place and switch chords by only moving two fingers. Finger 5 is already playing the note G, so leave it there. Finger 2 rests above the note D when you play the C Major chord, so you won't have to move it far down from E to D.

As you move your thumb down from the note C to the note B, you'll have everything in place to play the first inversion G Major chord!

Figure 5a shows these movements. Place your right hand on the root position C Major chord and practice moving from there to the first inversion G Major chord. Finger 5 will remain on the note G, so use it as an anchor point as you stretch your thumb down and place your 2nd finger to find the inverted G Major chord.

Figure 5a:

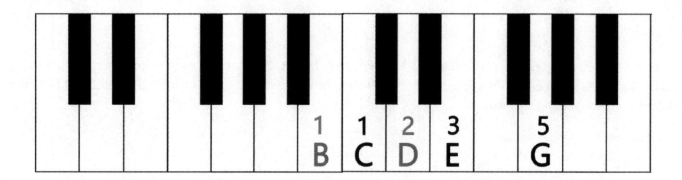

Once you can comfortably move between these two chords, play the following example to practice this move with your right hand. Even though you don't have to move your hand to reach the notes, it'll be easier to play if you use the lift and land technique between each chord and it will feel similar to playing a block chord accompaniment pattern.

Example 5i:

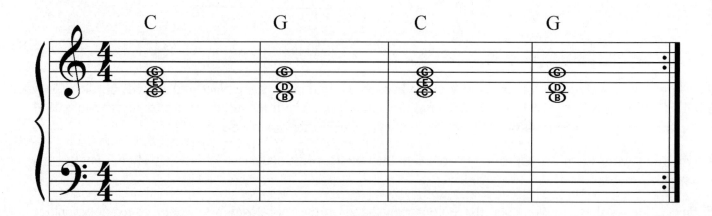

Now practice the same progression with the left hand. This will feel a little different because of the different chord fingerings. Figure 5b shows the correct fingering for the left hand.

Your thumb remains on the note G while the rest of your hand moves down to reach the notes B and D with fingers 3 and 5. Stretch from the thumb, using it as an anchor point as you reach down to find the other notes.

Practice this move slowly with the left hand as you get used to stretching your hand down to reach the inverted G Major chord and back up to play the root position C Major chord.

Figure 5b:

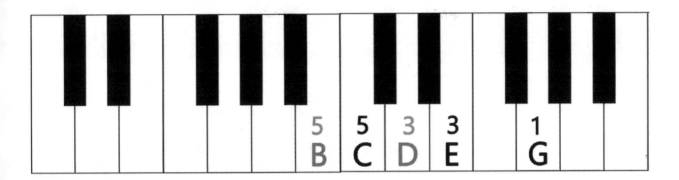

When you can make this move comfortably, play the following example.

Example 5j:

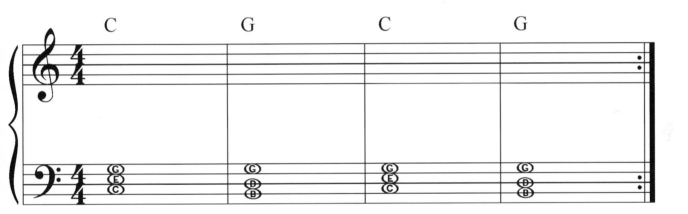

Remember to lift and land between chords even if it doesn't feel natural at first.

Notice how the note G acts as an anchor point to help you keep your place. Notes shared between chords are called *common tones*, and they are very useful when moving between inversions.

Let's use common tones to build our next progression with inversions: C Major to F Major. Figure 5c shows how using inversions and the common tone C creates a smooth transition between these two chords.

Figure 5c:

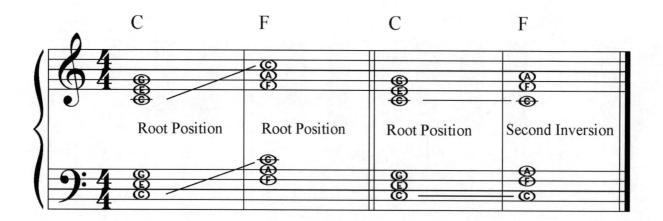

Using the note C as an anchor point and changing to F Major in second inversion allows you to play this progression without moving your hand across the keys. Play the inverted version of this progression with both right and left hands until you can move comfortably between the chords.

When you can easily find the notes of the F Major inversion, play Example 5k. Place both hands on C Major chords before you begin so that you're prepared.

Example 5k:

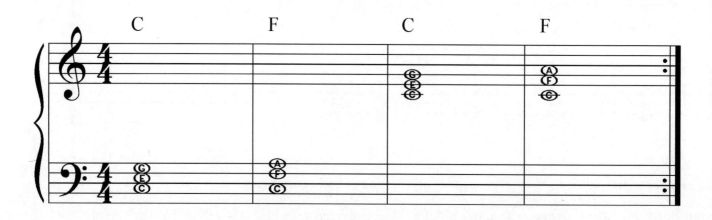

Many chords share at least one common tone, so you can use this approach as a handy shortcut when playing inversions. The only exceptions are chords that sit directly above or below any given chord. For example, the G Major chord does not have any common tones with F Major or A minor. When playing chords with no common tones, it's usually easiest to just move to the chord rather than looking for an inversion.

You have now learned about inversions and how to use common tones to find the best inversion for a progression. Let's put this into practice with some exercises.

Let's apply inversions to the I – vi – IV – V progression to create smoother voice leading. I have chosen and notated the inversions for you, using common tones to find the easiest moves between the chords.

Play this progression slowly on your own until you can easily find and move between all the inversions. Use the common tones as an anchor point to help you keep your place. Notice that the F Major and G Major chords do not have a common tone because they are adjacent chords, but the move is still easy because you move from the second inversion F Major chord to a second inversion G Major chord. All you have to do is move up one note in each finger to change chord.

When you can comfortably move between the chords on your own, play along with the audio. Lift your hand early if you need extra time to find the next chord. Take your time as you figure out the inversions and how to play them. If you forget what notes are in a chord, play it in root position to remind yourself what notes are in the chord and what it sounds like.

Example 5l:

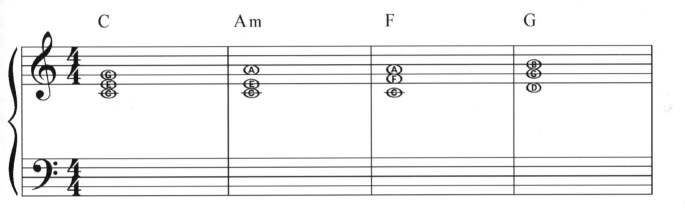

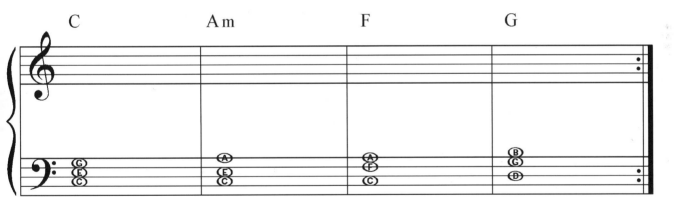

Let's play the inverted I – vi – IV – V progression with a broken accompaniment pattern. You can apply accompaniment patterns to inverted chords just as you do to root position chords. Play through the next example slowly at first and pay attention to the fingering for each inversion. When you can comfortably play it on your own, play along with the recording.

Example 5m:

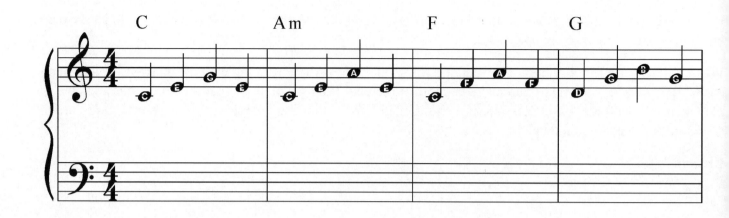

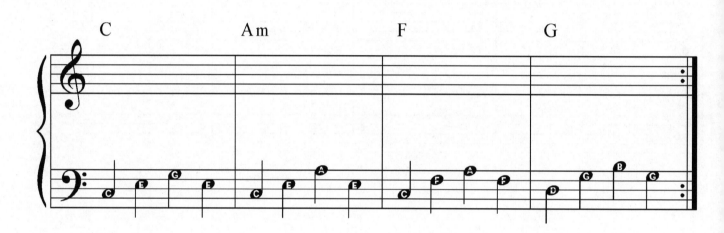

Inverted chords can be played with block chord accompaniments as well. Practice the following example to gain more experience with inversions and accompaniment patterns. Notice how inversions make playing accompaniment patterns easier because you don't have to move your hand up and down the keyboard.

Example 5n:

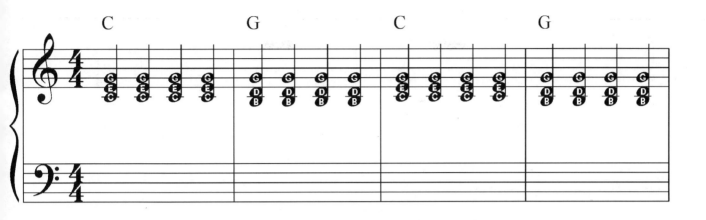

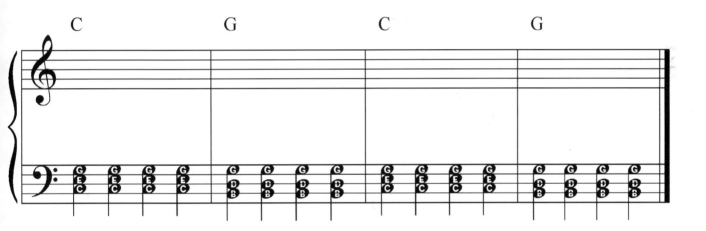

The rest of this book will use chord inversions in the songs. It can be difficult to know which inversion to use, so I will notate the smoothest voice leading for you to make playing easier. After some practice, you will develop a sense of which inversions create a smooth transition between chords. But for those of you who like to know how things work in further depth, let's go through the process one more time.

First, identify the notes in your chords. Then identify the common tones. Let's use C Major and E minor as an example. The C Major chord has the notes C, E and G, while E minor has the notes E, G and B. This chord set actually has two notes in common: E and G.

Once you have identified the common tones, use them as anchor points. These notes will stay the same so that you don't have to move your hand across the keys when you change chords. Since C Major and E minor have the notes E and G in common, the only change you need to make is to move the note C down a step to B.

Example 5o:

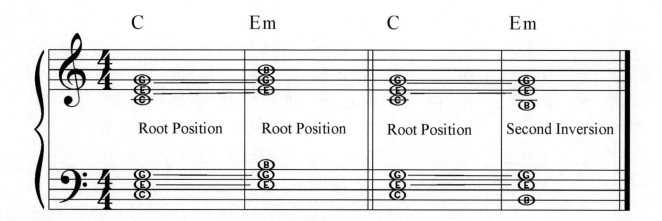

If you want more practice, go through the following pairs of chords. Identify the common tones, use those as an anchor point, and find an inversion that leads to a smooth voice leading.

C (C E G) and Em (E G B)

F (F A C and Dm (D F A)

Am (A C E) and F (F A C)

G (G B D) and C (C E G)

Em (E G B) and Am (A C E)

We've now covered some of the most important points of playing chords on piano: root position voicings, accompaniment patterns and inversions. In the next chapter we'll take a look at additional chord types to introduce new sounds into our music.

Chapter Six: Sus2 and Sus4 Chords

So far you have played major and minor chords. These are the foundation of most music, but there are many different ways to modify them to change the sound and make the music more interesting. One popular way to do this is with *suspended chords,* often called *sus* chords for short. Suspended chords replace the middle note of a chord with either the 2nd or 4th note up from the root.

Sus2 Chords

Example 6a shows a C Major chord compared to a Csus2 chord. When notating the sus2 chord on a lead sheet, the chord symbol will show the root of the chord with "sus2" after it.

To reate a Csus2 chord, replace the note E (the 3rd) with the note D (the 2nd). In other words, play the second note above C instead of the third. You should already have a finger hovering above the note D, so the substitution is easy.

Here's how that Csus2 chord sounds next to a regular C Major. Listen to how it has an unresolved or "suspended" quality. Often you'll hear pianists resolving that suspended 2nd note back up to the 3rd.

Example 6a:

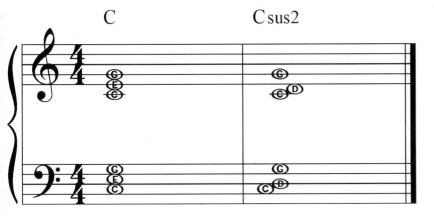

Example 6b shows you how to play Csus2 chords in both hands.

Use the lift and land technique as you repeat the chord and listen to the sound. Keep your fingers curved as you bring down your arm to play the notes. This is especially important for the left hand, as finger 4 is your weakest finger and will tend to collapse if you don't keep it curved. Find the Csus2 chord in different places on the piano, moving up and down the keyboard as you play.

Example 6b:

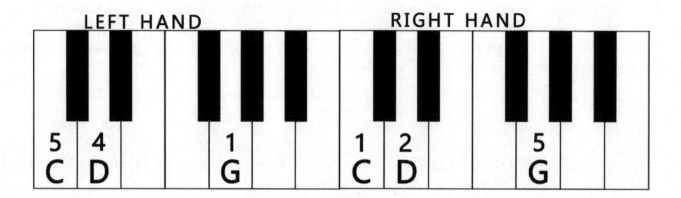

When you can comfortably play the previous idea, look at Example 6c. Place both hands on the C Major chord before you begin and perform the following block chord accompaniment pattern.

Example 6c:

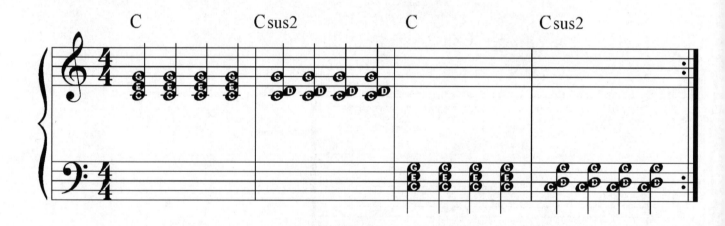

Now let's learn the other most common suspension: the sus4.

Sus4 Chords

As you might guess, in a sus4 chord the third note above the chord root is replaced with the fourth. In a C major chord, that means that you play the note F instead of the note E.

Example 6d:

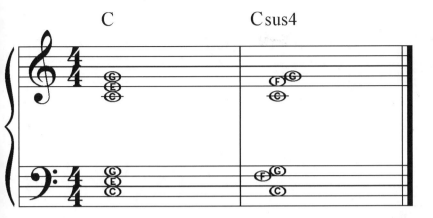

Sometimes you'll see a chord written as just "C sus". This normally means sus4 as this is the most common suspended chord type.

Example 6e shows the Csus4 chord fingerings for each hand. This time the right hand plays a note with finger 4, so keep your fingers curved so it does not collapse.

Practice playing the Csus4 chord with both hands until you can easily find and comfortably play it. Listen to how it sounds different from both the C Major and Csus2 chords. Play this chord at different places on the piano to explore how it sounds in the high and low registers.

Example 6e:

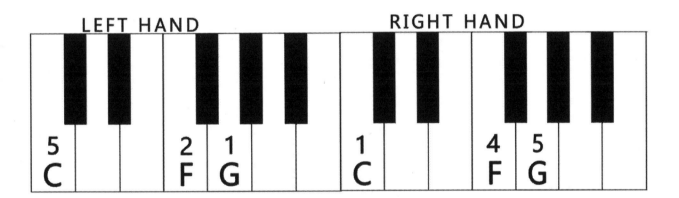

When you can comfortably play the Csus4 chord with both hands, try the next example.

Example 6f:

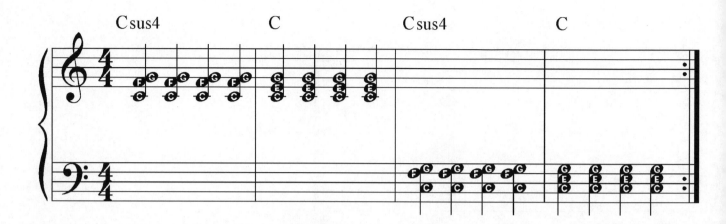

Did that example sound familiar? Moving from a sus4 chord to a major chord with the same root has been a popular progression for centuries. It's especially common in hymns and other sacred music, earning it the nickname the *amen cadence*. You can also hear it in modern songs like *Hard to Say I'm Sorry* (Chicago).

In Western classical music, the sus4 chord almost always resolves in this way, but many modern songs use suspended chords as a way to make the harmony more interesting. Modifying chords is a great way to add *color* to your harmony.

Songs that use suspended chords for color include *Love Song* (Sara Bareilles), *The Scientist* (Coldplay) and *100 Years* (Five for Fighting). There are also some iconic songs for guitar that use suspended chords. Some of my favorites are *Free Fallin'* (Tom Petty), *Black or White* (Michael Jackson) and *Pinball Wizard* (The Who).

Inverting Suspended Chords

Suspended chords can be inverted just like major and minor chords.

Example 6g:

Some suspended chords have the same notes, so it can be tricky to tell which chord you're playing when you invert the chords. For example, both Csus2 and Gsus4 chords have the notes C, D and G. So, a second inversion Csus2 chord looks just like a Gsus4 chord.

However, there's no need to worry about this or spend a lot of time trying to figure out which chord is which if you come across this situation. As long as you play the correct notes for the labeled chord, the music will sound right.

Example 6h:

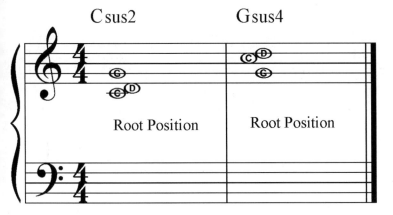

Let's practice making some music with suspended chords.

Exercise One

Play a D minor chord with your right hand. Using the process you have just learned let's play the sus2 and sus4 chords around D minor by moving the 3rd (middle note) up and down. This is shown in Example 6i. Learn the movements slowly, then play along with the audio. Since suspended chords are neither major nor minor, the suspensions are simply "Dsus2" rather than "Dminor sus2."

Remember to lift and land to make the repeated notes easier to play.

Example 6i:

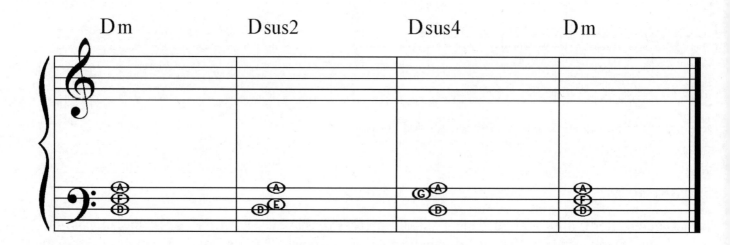

Exercise Two

Now let's play a song using suspended chords. The Csus2 and Dsus2 chords not only add color to the harmony, they also make the transitions to the inverted chords that follow them easier. If you find the music hard to follow, play these chords in root position or go back and review previous chapters to build more muscle memory for these chords.

Play this song slowly without the audio first. Take your time as you find all the chords and practice moving between them.

Example 6j:

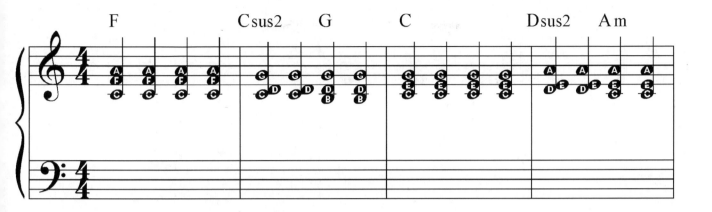

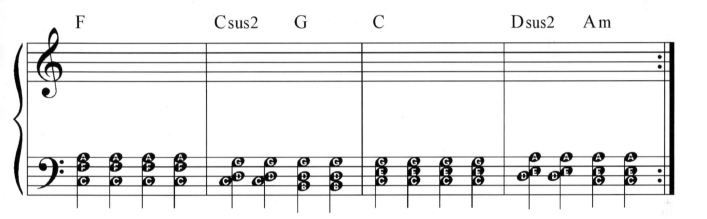

Exercise Three

Now let's try some sus4 chords with a broken chord accompaniment. When you can comfortably play this example with both hands, play along with the audio.

Example 6k:

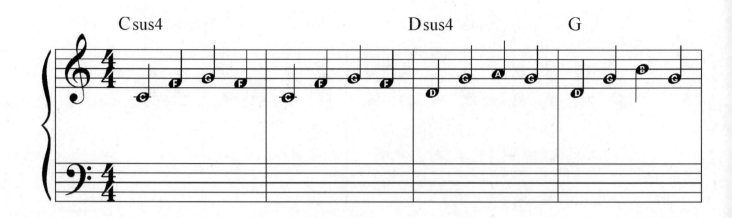

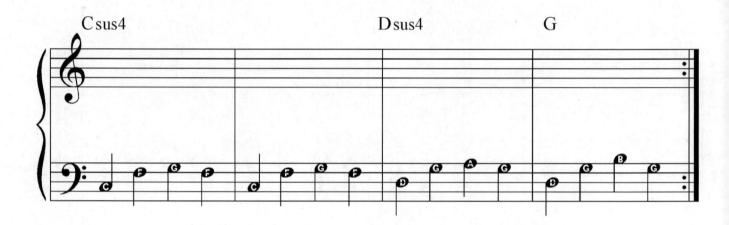

Exercise Four

Let's add suspended chords to the I-vi-IV-V progression to create a more colorful harmony. Listen to the track to hear how adding suspended chords changes the progression's sound. Play through the example slowly on your own, then play along with the track.

Example 6l:

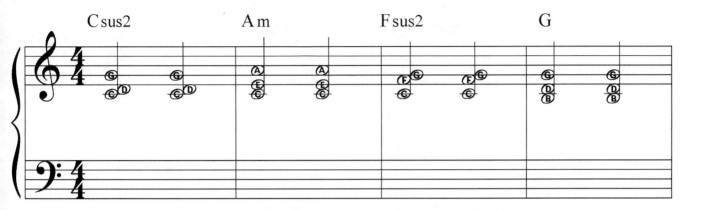

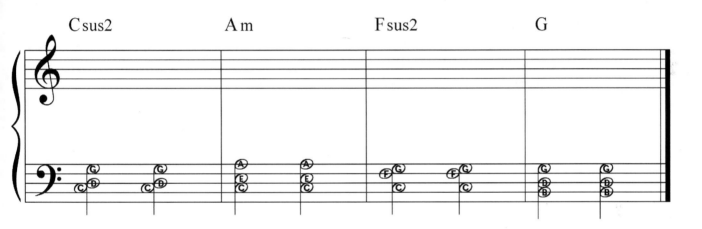

Congratulations! You have learned two more types of chords. If you want more experience with suspensions, go back and add them to previous examples using whatever combinations of sus2 and sus4 chords you like. Have fun discovering new sounds and making music that is uniquely yours.

Chapter Seven: Left Hand Bass Lines

So far you have played songs by switching chords between the right and left hands. I have all my students do this at first because it's the easiest way to learn the notes of the chord and build muscle memory. But more advanced pianists play different things with both hands at the same time and now you're ready to do the same!

An easy way to produce an interesting sound is to play a bass line with the left hand instead of a chord. This provides a stable foundation for your music, like adding a bass player to your band. Pianists have a great advantage when playing chords because they can play multiple parts at the same time!

Instead of three note chords, bass lines typically consist of just the root note of the chord. For the C Major chord, play the note C. For the A minor chord, play the note A etc.

So a bass line for a I-V-vi-IV progression in C Major would look like this:

Example 7a:

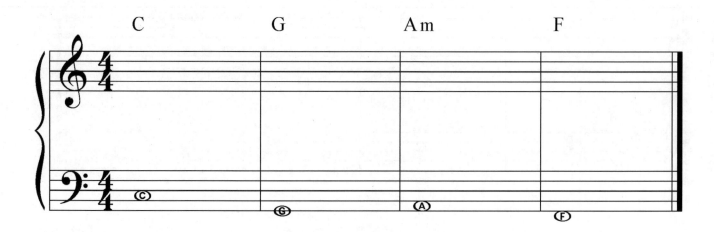

Place your left thumb on the note C, positioning your hand as if you were going to play an F Major chord. Then play the notes in Example 7a. You won't need to move your hand to reach the notes if you have positioned it correctly. Simply change the finger you play the note with.

Once you can comfortably play this bass line with the left hand, you're ready to add the right hand chords.

Practice the following example with each hand separately at first. Give your right hand plenty of time to learn this progression using the inversions. When you can comfortably play each hand on its own, play them together slowly. Remember that your left hand shouldn't need to move to play the bass line, you just need to switch fingers.

Example 7b:

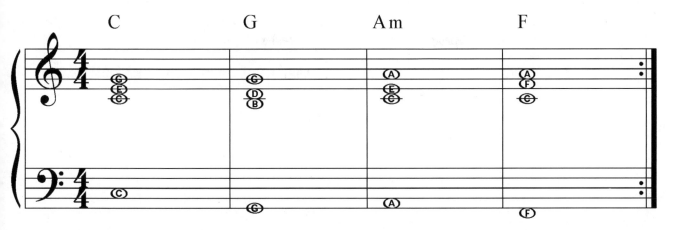

When you can easily play this example on your own, play along with the audio track. Remember that you can lift off the chord early with the right hand to find the next position if needed. Playing with both hands at the same time requires practice as you build muscle memory. Go slowly and have patience as you build this new skill.

If you struggle to play along with the audio using both hands together, play each hand separately with the audio a few times for extra practice. Playing with hands separate is a great practice strategy – it allows you to build muscle memory for each one more easily.

Let's now add a bass line to the I-vi-IV-V progression. This progression uses the same chords in a different order, so you will use the same hand positions. Place your right hand on the C Major chord and finger 1 of your left hand on C to begin.

Practice this example slowly with hands separate first. Once you can comfortably play each hand separately, put them together and practice until you have built muscle memory for this progression. When you're ready, play along with the audio.

Example 7c:

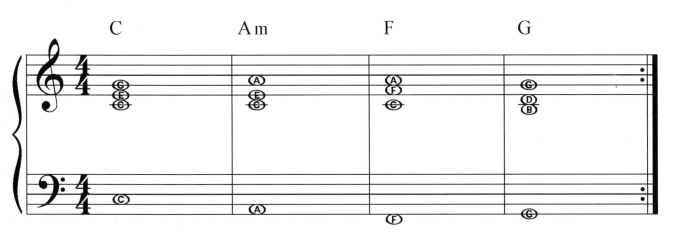

Bass Lines with Accompaniment Patterns

Left hand bass lines also work with the accompaniment patterns you have learned so far. In fact, they give you more options! Songs that use accompaniment patterns with simple left hand bass lines include *Rocket Man* (Elton John), *Back to Black* (Amy Winehouse) and *Someone Like You* (Adele).

Play the I-vi-IV-V progression using a broken chord accompaniment with root note bass line. Practice this example slowly on your own first, then play along with the audio.

Example 7d:

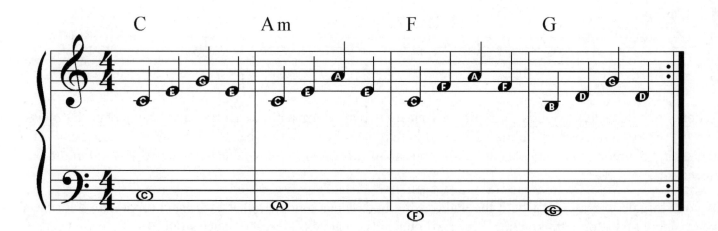

It may take some practice to be able to hold the left hand bass notes down while playing the broken chords with the right hand. For most of our daily activities, our hands do the same thing at the same time. You must teach them to work independently of each other.

The next example uses a left hand bass line with a block chord accompaniment in the right hand. Notice that the bass line does not change when you switch from the C major to the Csus2 or Csus4 chords because they all have the same root.

Example 7e:

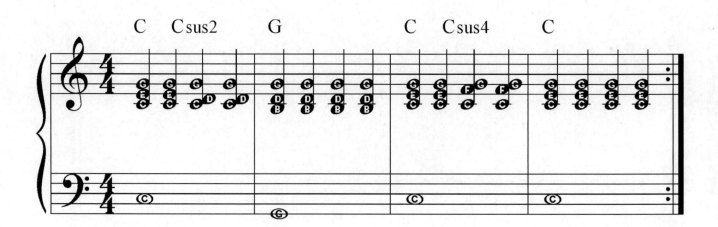

Once again, practice your hands separately first without the audio. Then put them together and practice slowly. When you can comfortably play this example on your own, play along with the audio.

Slash Chords

Bass lines often play a supporting role, but they can also be the stars of the song!

Examples of iconic bass lines include *Another One Bites the Dust* (Queen), *Let It Be* (The Beatles) and *I Want You Back* (The Jackson 5). Bass lines that don't follow the roots of the chords are notated in lead sheets with a *slash chord.*

A slash chord is shown by two letters divided by a slash symbol. The first letter shows which chord the right hand should play. The second letter shows which bass note the left hand should play. It's important to remember that the first letter represents a chord while the second represents only a single bass note. I have seen players get confused and play two different chords at the same time. That doesn't sound good!

The following figure shows the C Major chord in root position followed by two different slash chords that create a bass line. Place both hands on a C Major chord then play this example. The right hand will play the C Major chord three times while the left hand changes notes to play the different bass lines notated by the slash chords.

Play the left hand alone before you play hands together, noticing how the bass line fits with the rest of the music.

Example 7f:

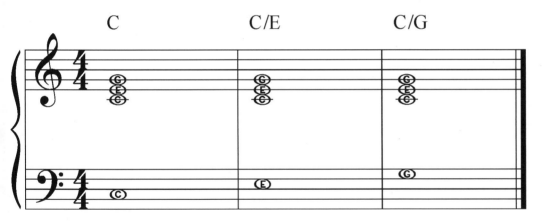

Slash chords can also be used to show a moving bass line under a sustained chord. The chord will stay the same, but the bass note changes underneath.

To play the example below, place your left hand with finger 1 on the note C, as if you were going to play an F Major chord.

Notice how the bassline steps down and back up again. Learn to play it in isolation, then play it with the audio track.

Once you can easily play the left hand bass line along with the audio, practice the right hand separately. Then put them together, playing slowly at first then increasing your speed. When you feel comfortable with the notes, play along with the audio track.

Notice how the moving bass line makes the chords sound more interesting. You can completely change the sound of the chords by changing the bass note underneath.

Example 7g:

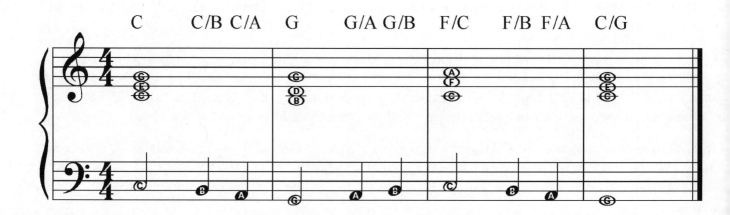

Changing bass lines is a great way to add interest to a progression as you repeat it. In the next example you will play the progression once with the standard bass line, then once with a more intricate slash chord bass part.

Place your left hand with finger 1 on C, as if you were going to play an F Major chord. Practice the bass line separately first to learn the notes, then put it together with the right hand chords.

Example 7h:

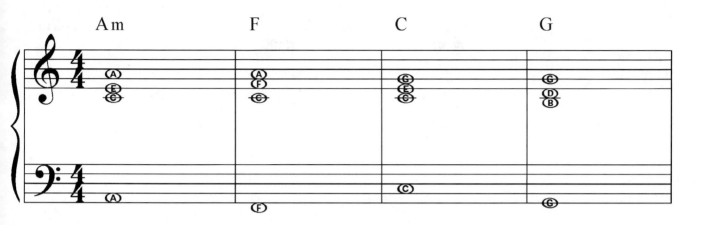

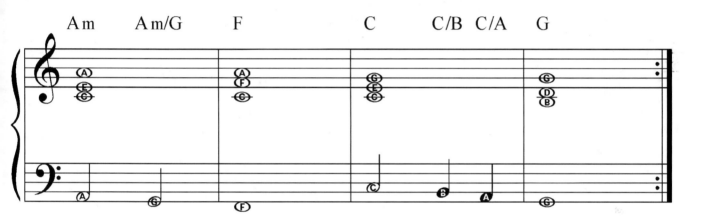

Repeating bass notes can add energy and drive to your music. This example uses the *'50s progression* with a popular bass line from that period. Listen to the audio first and you'll hear that this example has three beats per measure instead of four. Tap along on your lap to feel the beat of the music before you play it on the piano.

When you understand the beat, learn the bass line. Once again, your left hand will be placed with finger 1 on the note C as if you were going to play an F Major chord. This bass line uses a combination of repeated notes and slash chords to create an interesting accompaniment that drives the music forward.

Once you can play the bass line, learn the right hand chords. Notice that you play each chord twice and hold it for three beats.

When you can play each part separately, play the hands together slowly on your own. Then play along with the audio.

Example 7i:

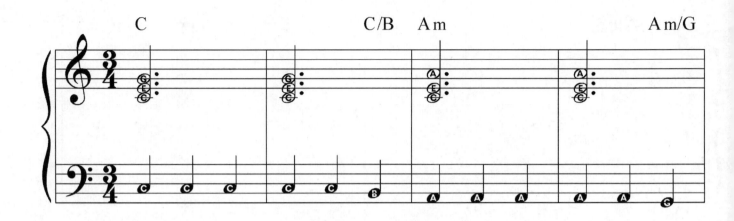

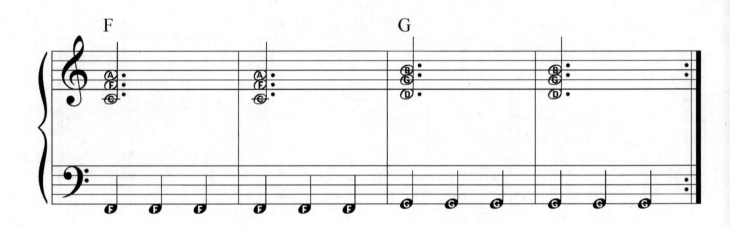

Another way to use slash chords is to hold a steady bass line while changing the chords above it. This is yet another way you can use a bass line to create a different musical feel.

Practice the right hand first until you can easily play the inversions with the broken chord accompaniment pattern. Then place left hand finger 1 on the note C and practice the left hand bass line.

Play them together slowly, then play along with the audio.

Example 7j:

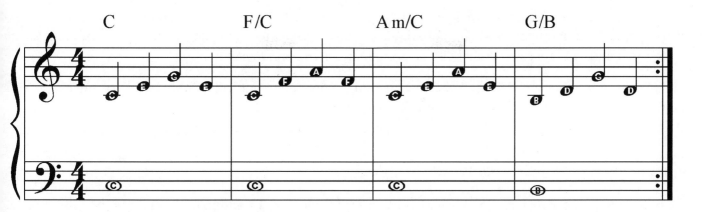

Now it's over to you. Take all the chord progressions you've learned so far and see if you can apply the techniques shown in this chapter to all of them.

Chapter Eight: Seventh Chords

You have learned four different types of chord: major, minor, sus2 and sus4. All of these chords are *triads*, meaning they contain three notes. But not all chords have three notes, and adding extra notes offers a wider variety of sounds and tone colors that can result in more interesting music.

Seventh chords are four-note chords based on extending major and minor triads. To create a seventh chord, you count up the scale from the root of the chord and add the seventh note.

Different Types of Seventh Chords

The following figure shows a seventh chord built on a C Major triad. Counting up from the note C, the seventh note is B.

Example 8a:

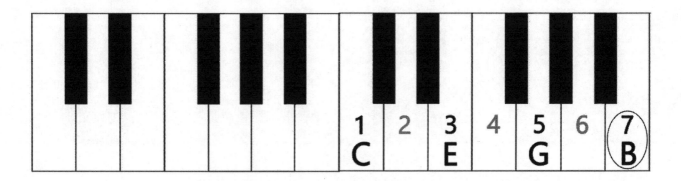

Seventh chords have a very cool, modern sound. They are used a lot in jazz, but are also popular in most musical genres and have been used for hundreds of years. There are four common types of seventh chords: major 7, minor 7, dominant 7 and minor 7 flat 5. We'll use the first three types in this book and save the minor 7 flat 5 for another time.

The reason that there are so many different types of seventh chords is beyond the scope of this book, but the simple explanation is that it depends on whether you start with a minor or major triad, and if the 7th is a major 3rd or a minor 3rd above the fifth of the triad. It gets a bit complicated and technical, and you don't need to know all the theory behind it to play the chords.

So let's play some chords!

The chord shown in Example 8a is a major 7 chord (a major chord with a major 3rd above the 5th, for those who are curious). Major 7 chords are shown in lead sheets by adding "Maj7" after the root of the chord, so this chord will be written as "CMaj7." This can also be abbreviated as "M7," an uppercase "M" with the number 7.

Example 8b:

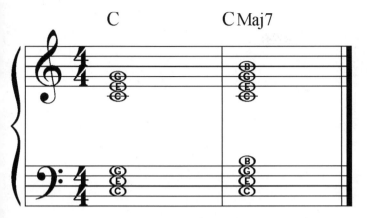

Let's build another seventh chord, this time using the note A as our root. The seventh note up from A is G, so you will add the note G to create the seventh chord. This is a minor 7 chord (a minor chord with a minor 3rd above the 5th).

Example 8c:

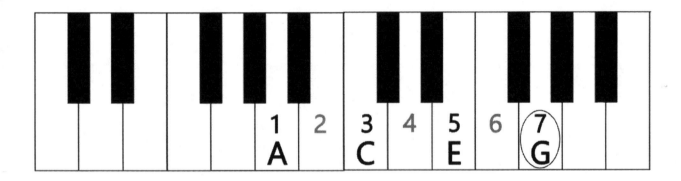

To show a minor 7 chord in a lead sheet, add "m7" to the root. So the minor 7 chord based on the note A is written as "Am7."

Example 8d:

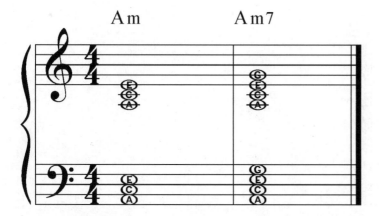

Can you hear the difference in sound between the major 7 and minor 7? Like major and minor triads, each seventh chord has a distinct sound that you can use to create interesting harmonies in your music.

Let's look at one more type of seventh chord: the dominant 7 (a major chord with a minor 3rd above the 5th). We'll build this chord on the note G. Listen to the recording of the dominant 7 chord and notice how it sounds different from the major 7 and minor 7.

Example 8e:

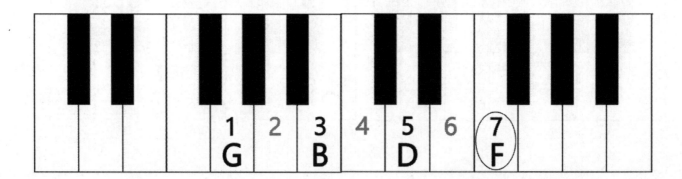

The dominant 7 chord is shown in lead sheets by simply adding "7" to the root. So a dominant 7 chord built on the note G is written as "G7."

Example 8f:

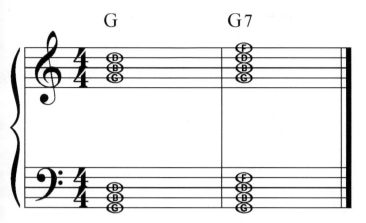

Playing Seventh Chords

When playing seventh chords with one hand, the extra note requires you to stretch your fingers to reach. Even if you have a large hand, this is not very comfortable. It's much easier to split the notes of the seventh chord between both hands, playing the root as a left hand bass line and the rest of the chord with the right hand.

Play the chords and bass lines shown in Example 8g. You are still playing the notes of the seventh chords even though you have split the notes between the hands. The root note has been moved to a lower octave to create a more interesting bass line, but it is still the root of the chord.

Example 8g:

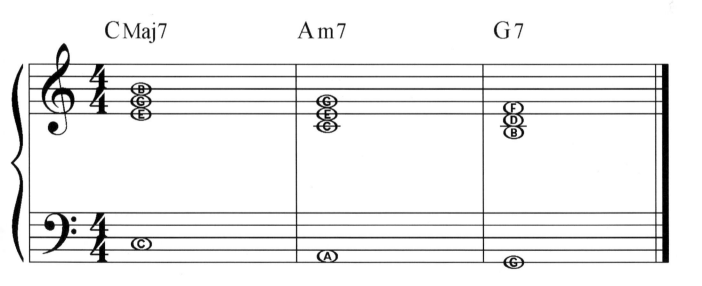

Notice that the right hand plays the notes of an E minor chord, but adding the C as a bass line changes the chord to a CMaj7 chord. For the Am7 chord, your right hand plays the notes of the C Major chord. For the G7 chord, the right hand plays a triad built on the note B (this chord is called a diminished triad for those who are curious). When playing seventh chords with the left hand taking the root as a bass line, the right hand always plays a triad that is three notes above the root.

Knowing this makes it easier to play seventh chords, as they are built around chords you already know. To figure out the notes of a seventh chord, find the root of the chord with your left hand, then count up three piano keys and build a triad with your right hand.

Let's play a song using seventh chords.

The following example uses the I – vi – IV – V progression, but all the chords have been changed to seventh chords. Listen to the audio first and notice how the progression sounds different with the seventh chords. Practice the example on your own, then play along with the audio track.

Example 8h:

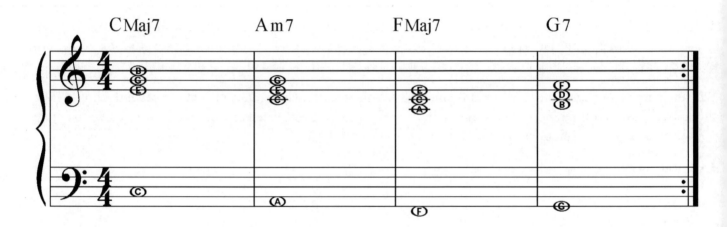

You can invert seventh chords to make them easier to play. The next example uses the same progression as Example 8h, but uses inverted chords so that the right hand doesn't have to jump around the keyboard.

Example 8i:

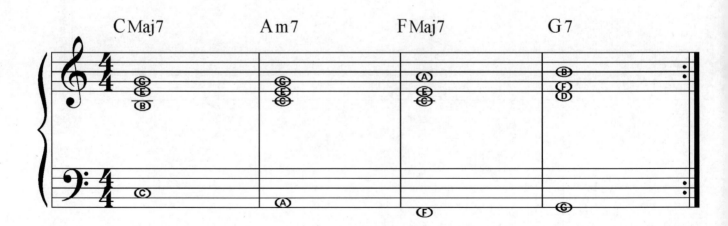

Let's look at more seventh chords in the key of C Major. Play through the chords in Example 8j to review the process for building seventh chords. Remember that the left hand will play the root while the right hand plays the triad, three notes above the root in the higher octave. Notice which triads combine with the different bass notes to form the seventh chords.

Example 8j:

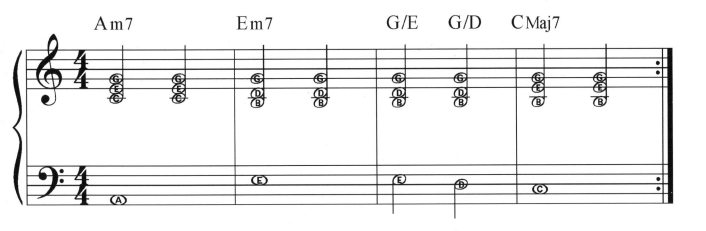

Let's play another song using seventh chords. This time you will use a basic accompaniment pattern as well.

Place finger 1 of your left hand on the note E as if you were going to play an A minor chord. Practice the bass line first, then learn the right hand on its own until you can comfortably play the inversions. When you're ready, play the hands together slowly on your own, then play along with the audio.

Example 8k:

Now let's add interest to the vi – IV – I – V progression by using seventh chords and a slash chord.

Example 81:

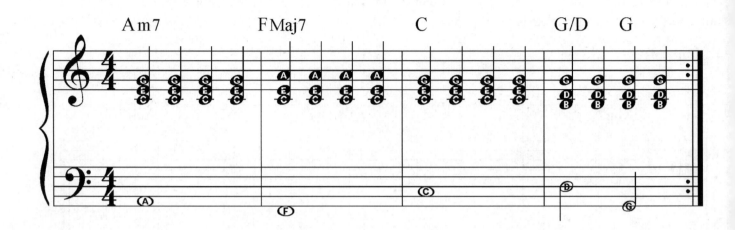

If you want more experience playing with seventh chords, go back to previous chapters and add 7th chords to all the progressions you've played so far. Start off by playing everything in root position with the bass note in the left hand before exploring inversions and slash chords.

In the next chapter, you'll learn how to combine everything you've learned and play more complex accompaniment patterns.

Chapter Nine: More Accompaniment Patterns

You can play thousands of songs with the progressions and accompaniment patterns you have already learned, but there are even more possibilities you can use to get creative and add variation to your music. In this chapter, you will learn some more advanced accompaniment patterns to give you even more options.

These can all be mixed and matched with what you have already learned. The only limit is your imagination.

Waltz Accompaniment Pattern

Let's learn a *waltz* accompaniment first. This pattern is named after the waltz dance, which has been popular for hundreds of years. You can hear waltz accompaniment patterns in such songs as *Piano Man* (Billy Joel), *You're the Reason* (Calum Scott) and *Here We Go* (Jon Brion).

Waltzes are characterized by a three-beat pattern with a strong first beat. The following example shows the basic waltz pattern on a C Major chord.

Example 9a:

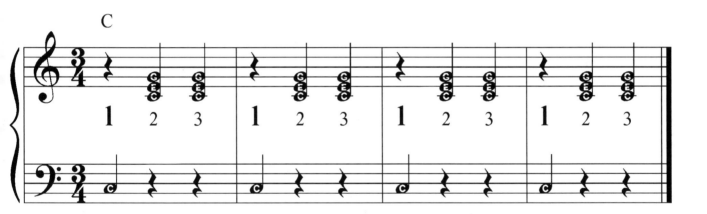

Play this example. Make sure you give extra emphasis to the bass note on beat one.

Now let's play a progression using the waltz accompaniment. Place your left-hand finger 1 on the note C as if you were going to play an F Major chord. Practice the bass line and chords separately, then put them together slowly.

Emphasize beat one as you play to give the music a strong waltz feel.

Example 9b:

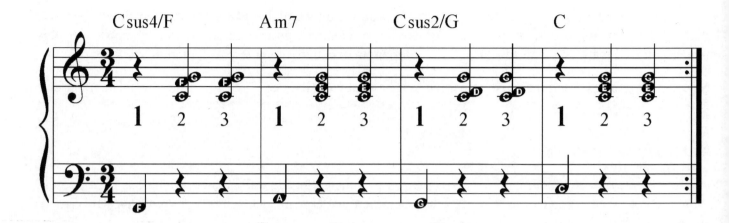

You can use this accompaniment pattern with any chord progression you have already learned or any that you learn in the future.

Rocking Accompaniment Pattern

Now let's learn the *rocking* chord accompaniment. This is a very popular accompaniment style and can be heard in songs like *Don't Stop Believin'* (Journey), *Imagine* (John Lennon) and *Beautiful* (Christina Aguilera).

As the name suggests, your hand will rock back and forth as you switch between different notes of the triad in the right hand to break the chord apart. You'll play the top two notes of the chord together and the bottom note of the chord on its own.

The following example shows a rocking chord pattern with the C Major chord.

Example 9c:

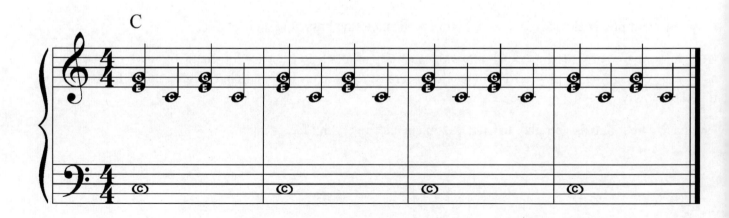

Do not try to play this pattern by only moving your fingers. Instead, keep your right hand loose and rotate from the wrist to create the rocking motion. The motion will be small, but it's an important thing to get right.

Let's try this accompaniment pattern with the I-V-vi-IV chord progression. Practice the right hand alone first as you master playing the rocking chord accompaniment pattern with inversions. Then place finger 1 of your left-hand on the note C and add the bass line. When you can comfortably play with your hands together slowly, play along with the audio.

Example 9d:

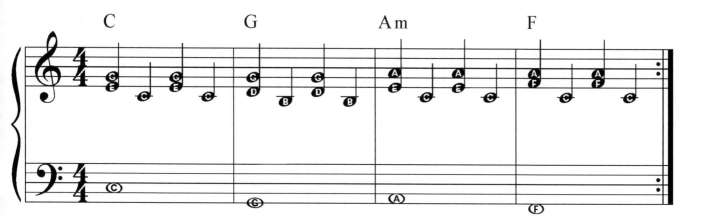

This is a versatile accompaniment pattern that's suitable for rock anthems, soulful ballads, and everything in between. The speed at which you play your rocking chords dramatically alter the musical effect.

Try it with a faster motion and notice how this adds more energy to the music.

Relaxation is the key to playing quickly. Keep loose because tension will slow you down.

Example 9e:

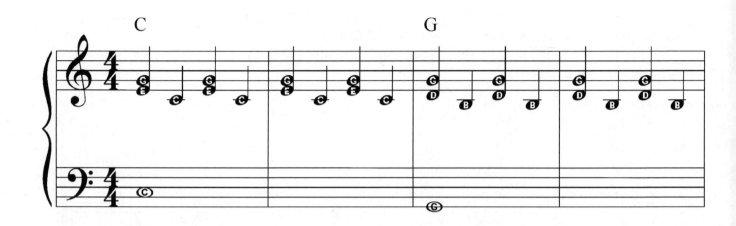

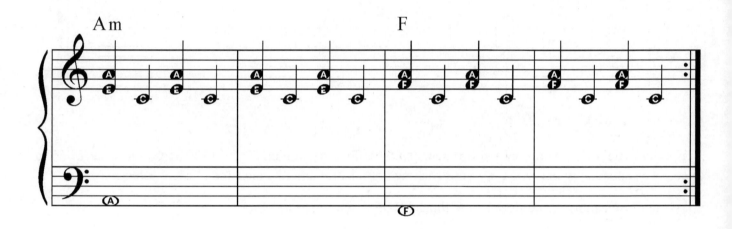

Combining Accompaniment Patterns

Combining accompaniment patterns is a great way to create a unique feel in your music. You can hear it in such songs as *7 Years* (Lukas Graham), *Tiny Dancer* (Elton John) and *100 Years* (Five for Fighting).

There are endless ways to combine the accompaniment patterns you have learned. The following example uses alternating blocked and broken accompaniment patterns. Notice that the last measure is marked "NC" which stands for "No Chord". This symbol is used in lead sheets to show that you should play something else such as a lead line or interesting melody. In this example, simply play the melody I've written.

Listen to the audio first to hear how this all fits together and practice in the normal way.

Example 9f:

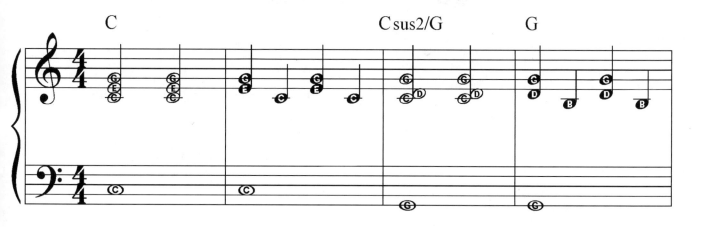

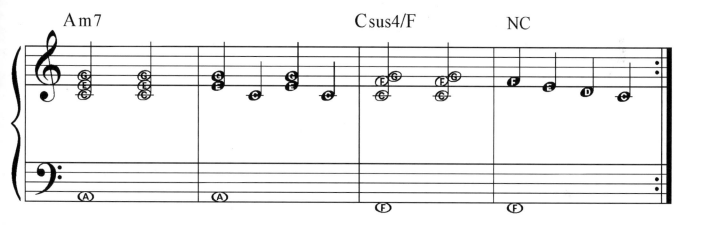

Let's put these three new accompaniment patterns into practice with more songs.

First, let's play another song with a waltz accompaniment. Remember to emphasize the bass note, which is beat one in the group of three.

Example 9g:

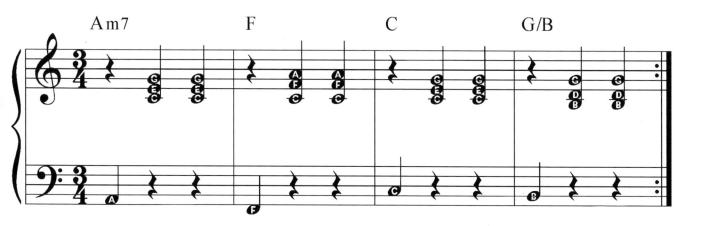

The next exercise uses a rocking accompaniment pattern and a moving bass line notated with slash chords. Notice how the different bass notes change the sound of the C Major chord on the first line and make it more interesting.

Example 9h:

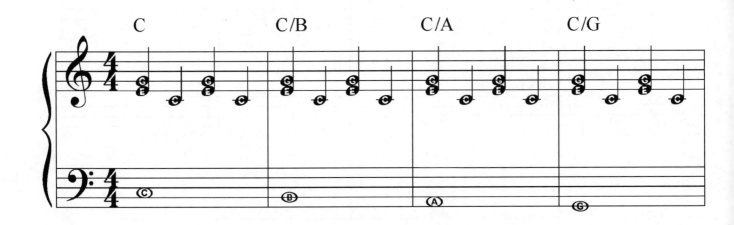

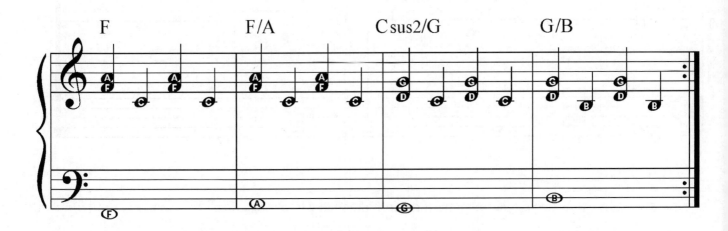

Now let's try another combination. In this example, we'll return to the first two accompaniment patterns you learned: blocked chords and broken chords. Listen to audio first and notice how the left hand and right hand parts fit together.

Example 9i:

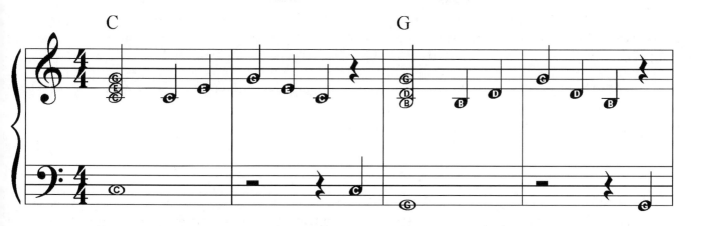

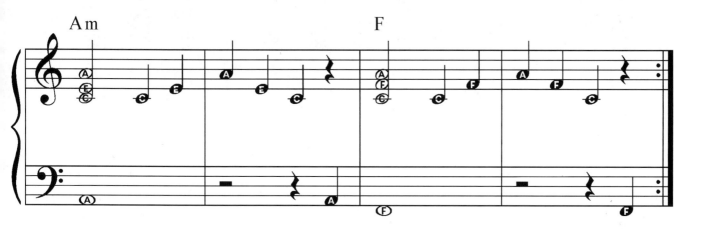

Congratulations! You've come a long way and can play several great accompaniment patterns. Not only that, you've started to combine them to create original ideas to use in your own rhythm parts.

Now you're ready to apply everything you have learned so far to a new key: the key of G Major.

Chapter Ten: The Key of G

Not every song is in the key of C, so the next step is to learn to play chords in different keys. We'll start with the key / scale of G Major. Like chords, keys are named after their first note. So the G Major scale is based on the note G.

The key of G Major has one black key: F#. The following figure shows the notes of the G Major scale. These are the notes you will use to build chords in G Major.

Figure 10a:

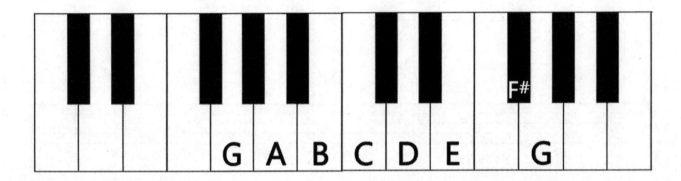

In music, the "#" symbol is called a "sharp". So you read "F#" as "F sharp". This symbol tells musicians to play the key directly to the right of the named key. The following figure shows a few more sharps to help you understand how they work.

Figure 10b:

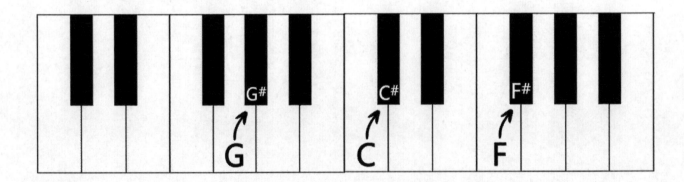

Let's play the the I – vi – IV – V progression in the key of G Major.

Because we're in the kcy of G, each Roman numeral now stands for a different chord.

G Major = I

C Major = IV

D Major = V

E minor = vi

The following image shows why the chords have changed. G is the first note of the scale now, so it becomes I. The rest of the chords are labeled based on the scale as well.

Figure 10c:

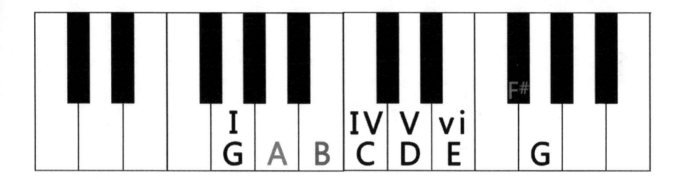

Let's take a closer look at the V chord.

The key of C Major contained a D minor chord which contains the note F. But because the key of G contains an F#, this changes the D chord to a major sound.

The following figures show the difference between the D minor and D Major chords on the keyboard

Figure 10d:

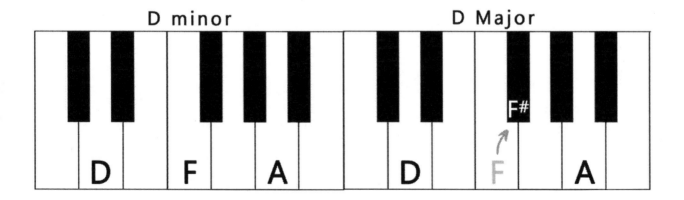

Listen to Example 10a to hear the difference between the major and minor chords.

Example 10a

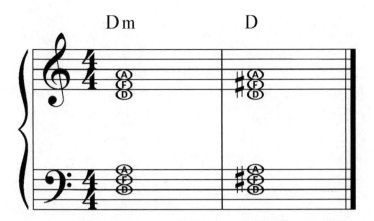

Practice playing D Major and notice how it sounds and feels different from D minor. When you play a chord that contains a black key, move your hand away from you and towards the instrument until you can comfortably reach the black key. Don't straighten your fingers to stretch for the key. Keep your fingers curved as you play and move your arm forward until your hand is in a comfortable position to reach all the notes.

Now that you can play the D Major chord, you're ready to play the I – vi – IV – V progression in the key of G Major. Play it in root position first. Put your left hand finger 1 on the note G as if you were going to play a C Major chord. This will enable you to play the bass line without moving your hand.

Example 10b:

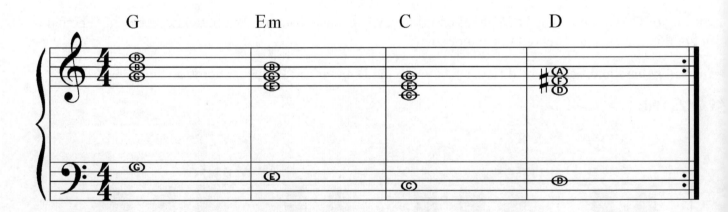

Now let's play the same progression with inversions. Practice the right hand part by itself first until you can comfortably play the inversions in the new key, then add the left hand bass line and play it with the track. Finger 5 is your shortest finger, so you will need to move your hand further into the keys to comfortably position it over the F#.

Example 10c:

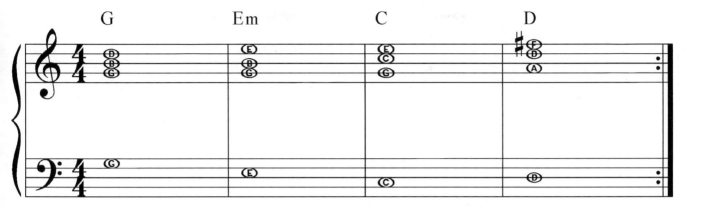

Congratulations! You have played your first song in the key of G Major. The best way to get comfortable with playing in a new key is to practice, so let's learn more songs in G Major and add in accompaniment patterns that you've already studied.

This exercise takes an example from Chapter 9 and moves it from the key of C to the key of G. Notice how it sounds similar, but the music is higher now. Watch out for the D Major chord inversion in the second measure – your thumb is shorter and shaped differently than the rest of your fingers, so you will need to move your hand into the keys quite a bit and lift slightly to find a comfortable playing position.

Example 10d:

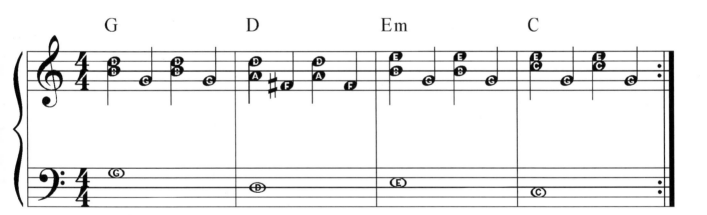

Let's give your left hand a chance to play something more interesting. Place left hand finger 1 on the note G and bring your hand into the keys so that finger 2 can easily reach the F#.

Example 10e:

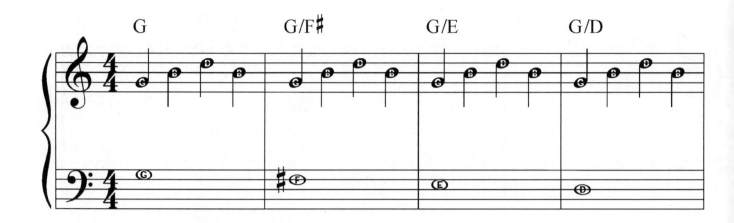

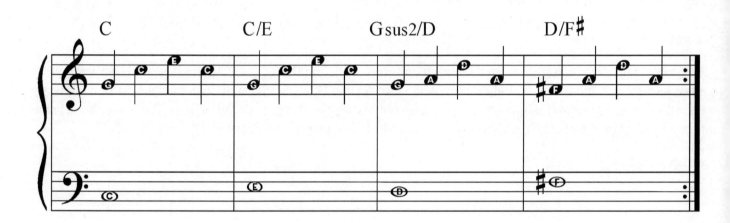

Everything you learned while playing in the key of C applies to the key of G, and you build chords the same way no matter what key you're playing in. Let's play an example that uses suspended chords.

Example 10f:

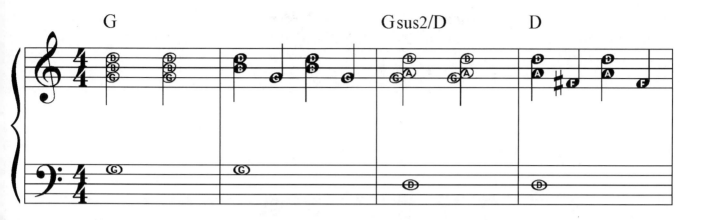

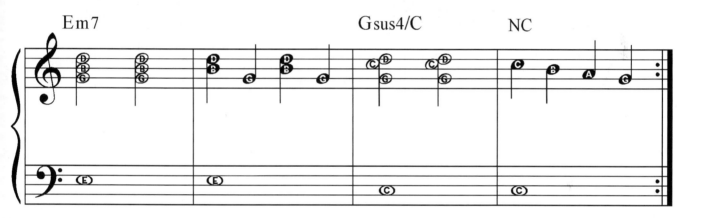

Congratulations! You can now play songs in the key of G!

Chapter Eleven: The Key of F

F Major is another popular musical key. As with the keys of C and G, playing in the key of F means that F is now your most important note, the F Major chord is your main chord, and you will use a different set of notes when building chords.

The following figure shows the notes used in the key of F.

Figure 11a:

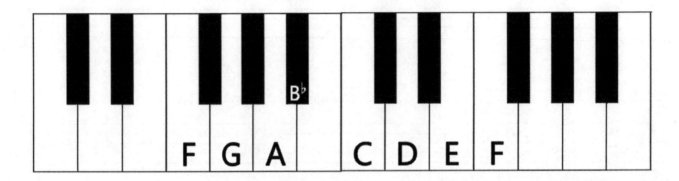

Notice that the key of F Major contains a Bb. In music, the symbol *"b"* is called a "flat" and tells you to move the indicated note down a half step. That is, play the key directly to the left, whether it's a white or black key.

The following image shows a few flats and the note that they are named after.

Figure 11b:

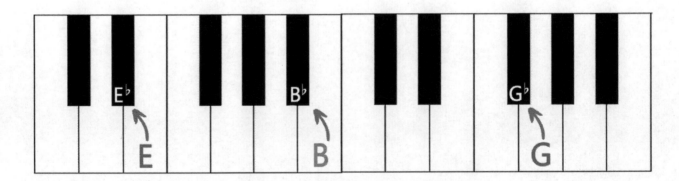

Let's play the the I – vi – IV – V progression in the key of F Major. Because we're in the key of F, each roman numeral now stands for a different chord.

F Major = I

B*b* Major = IV

C Major = V

D minor = vi

Figure 11c:

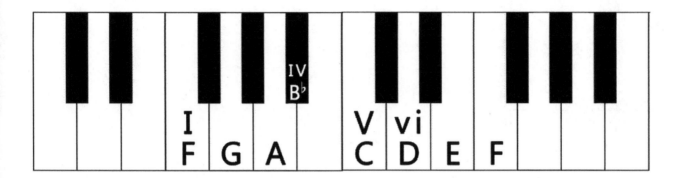

The only new chord in this progression is Bb Major. Let's learn that chord to prepare for playing the progression.

Bb Major starts on a black key, but you still follow the same process to build and play the chord.

Because fingers 1 and 5 are your shortest fingers and the black keys are shorter than the white keys, you will need to move your hand further into the keys as you did with the D Major chord. Move your entire arm from your shoulder until your hand is comfortably hovering over the notes of the chord. Do not try to stretch your fingers to reach.

The following figure shows the notes of the Bb chord. Play it with both hands until you feel comfortable with the notes.

Example 11a:

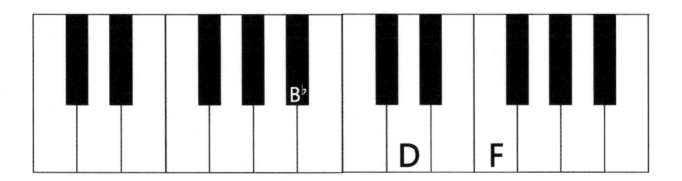

The following figure shows how the Bb Major chord looks in sheet music and with a lead sheet. Play this chord a few more times, moving up and down the piano as you get used to how it feels to play a chord with a black key as the root.

Example 11b:

Once you have mastered the Bb Major chord, you're ready to play the I – vi – IV – V progression in the key of F Major.

For the left hand bass line, place finger 1 on the note F and move your hand into the keys until finger 5 can comfortably rest on the Bb.

Practice with the hands separate, then put them together and practice slowly, then play along with the audio.

Example 11c:

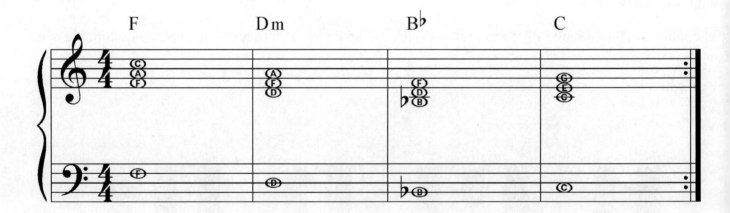

One you can play this progression using root position chords, you're ready to play it with inversions.

Practice the right hand separately until you can comfortably play the inverted chords, then put the hands together and play along with the track. Notice that when the Bb Major chord is inverted, finger 3 plays the Bb instead of finger 1, so you won't need to move your hand as far forward to reach the notes.

Example 11d:

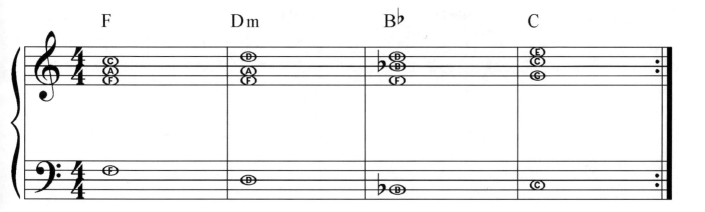

Congratulations! You have played your first song in F Major. Let's play some more. Example 11e uses a previous example that has been put into the new key. As you play it, notice what feels different and what feels the same.

Example 11e:

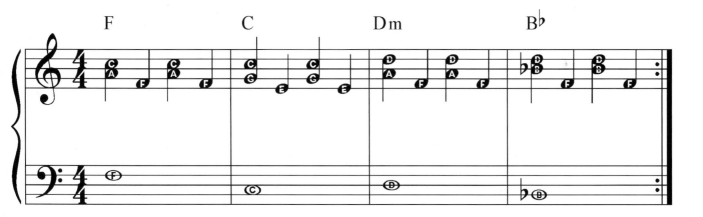

Let's once again give your left hand a chance to play a more interesting bass line in the new key. You've already played this example in the key of G, but the key of F can be challenging for the left hand because finger 5 is placed on the Bb. Move your arm away from your body and make sure that left hand finger 5 is comfortably placed over the Bb before you play the example.

Example 11f:

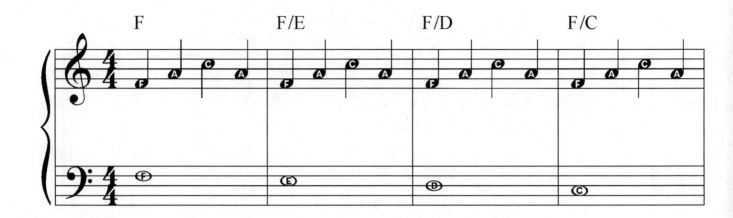

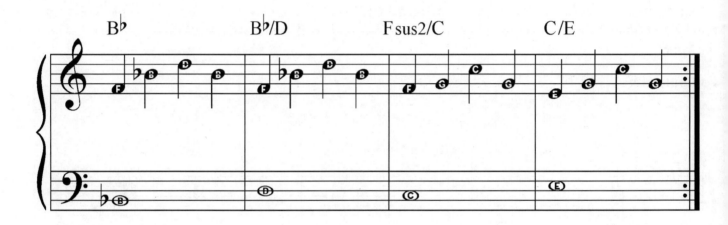

As I've mentioned, sus and seventh chords are built in the same way no matter what key you play in. Notice that you'll have a black key in the Fsus4 chord. Bring your hand forward so that finger 4 doesn't have to stretch to reach.

Example 11g:

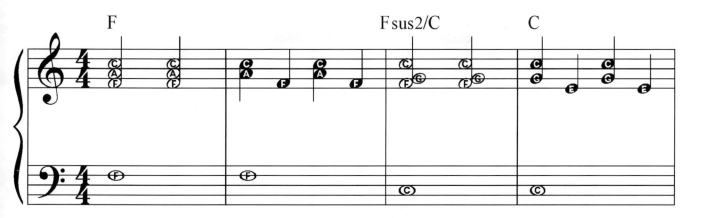

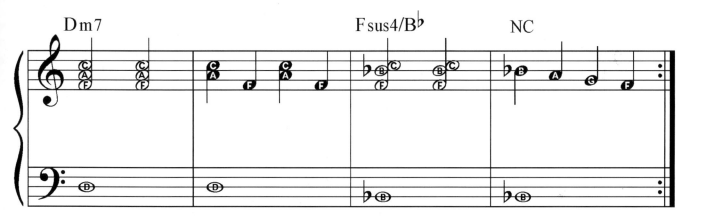

You can now play music in three different keys! In the final chapter, we'll apply everything you've learned to more advanced songs.

Chapter Twelve: Advanced Songs

Are you ready for the final chapter? You've learned a lot and now it's time to play! Let's explore more piano styles and advanced chord techniques.

The 12-Bar Blues

We'll start with the blues. There are many different blues styles and the style itself encourages improvisation and experimentation. I'll walk you through a few variations.

First, let's learn a blues progression. The most common is the *12-bar blues*. As the name suggests, this progression is twelve measures long. In its most basic form, it uses the I, IV and V chords, although numerous variations are possible. You can hear this progression in blues songs like *What'd I Say* (Ray Charles), *Money Blues* (Camille Howard) and *I Feel Good* (James Brown), but it is used also in songs outside of blues such as *Birthday* (Beatles) and *Still Haven't Found What I'm Looking For* (U2).

Listen to the 12-bar blues in Example 12a, then practice on your own and play along with the recording. This example is in the key of C Major.

Example 12a:

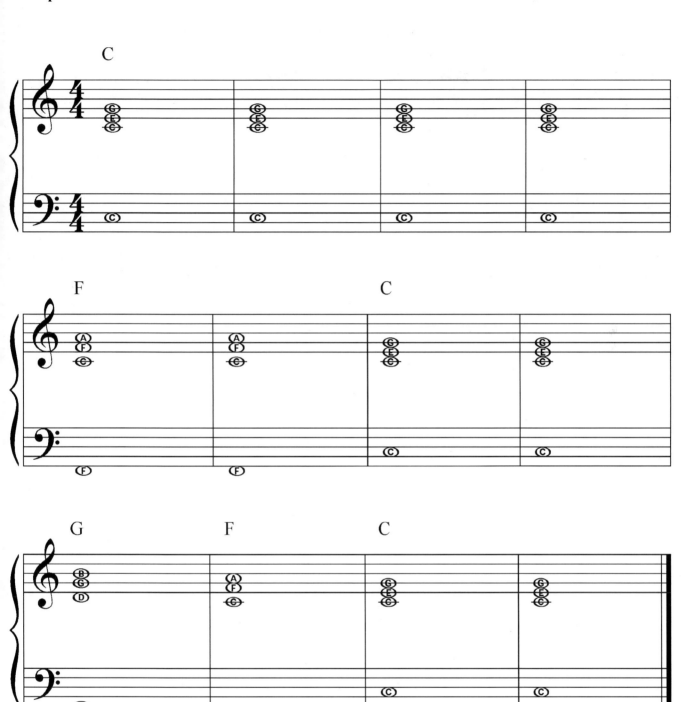

Let's make the harmony more interesting by using seventh chords! It is typical to use dominant seventh chords for this type of progression, so that's exactly what the next example does. To create dominant seventh chords in the key of C Major, you have to add some flats. Listen to the recording and carefully note which keys are flat in the following example. Trust your ear as you play and use it to help you identify and correct any wrong notes.

Example 12b:

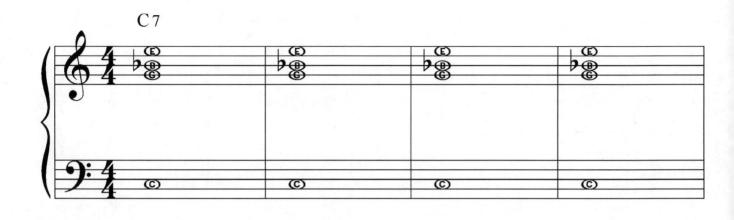

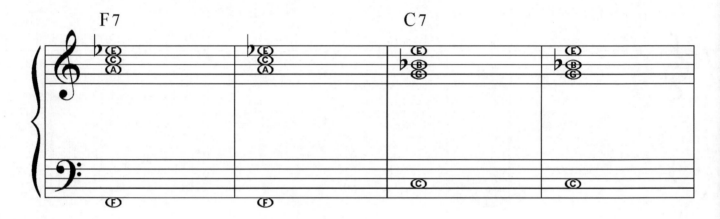

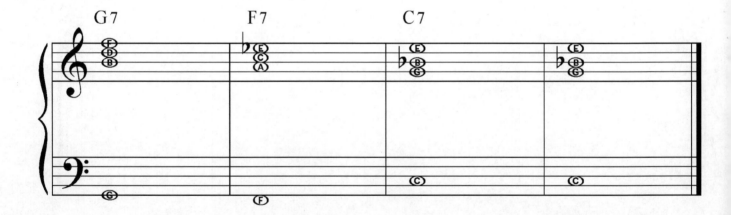

Now let's play the same progression in the key of F Major. We'll once again use dominant seventh chords for a more interesting sound. This example also uses repeating notes in the bass to add more rhythmic drive.

94

Example 12c:

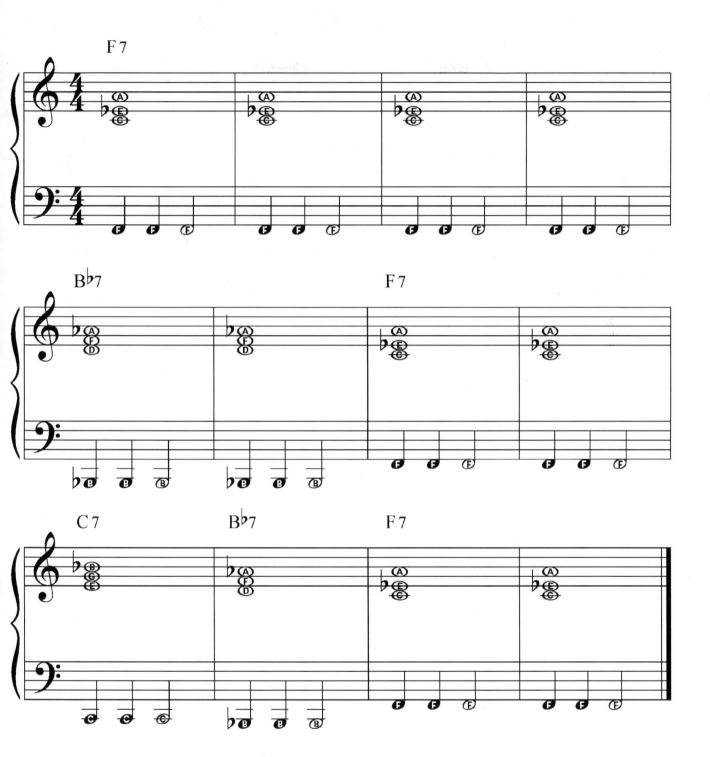

Let's return to the easier right hand part and give the left hand a challenge with a *walking bass line*. While the bass player would play this in a band, pianists can play both parts by themselves!

Rather than playing a single note or slash chord bassline as we have done so far, the left hand will outline the chord with a broken chord accompaniment pattern. This is a very popular bass pattern for the blues. Notice that you will need to move your left hand to the root position of each chord that you play to reach the notes of the walking bass line. Use the lift and land technique and focus on finding the root of the chord first as you move.

Play the left hand part slowly by itself at first. It may take some practice to make the moves between chords. When you can easily play both hands together on your own, play this example along with the track. When you feel comfortable with the example, move your left hand lower on the piano to get an even deeper bass sound. Relax and have fun as you play!

Example 12d:

Let's play one more blues example. This one is in the key of G Major and uses both seventh chords and a more complex walking bass line to make the music sound even more interesting. Use fingers 5, 3, 2 and 1 to play the notes of this walking bass line. Work slowly through this example, using the recording and the sheet music to help you as you learn the notes. This example is more difficult than anything we've done so far and may take some time to learn. Have patience as you put the pieces together.

Example 12e:

Key Changes and Borrowed Chords

Sometimes songs change key midway or borrow chords from other keys for dramatic effect. You can hear this in songs such as *Love on Top* (Beyonce), *I Will Always Love You* (Whitney Houston) and *Wouldn't It Be Nice* (Beach Boys).

Let's play some songs with key changes! Example 12f uses chords from the key of F Major in the first line then switches to the same progression with chords in the key of G Major in the second line. Pay careful attention to the D minor and D Major chords, as you play both in this song.

Example 12f:

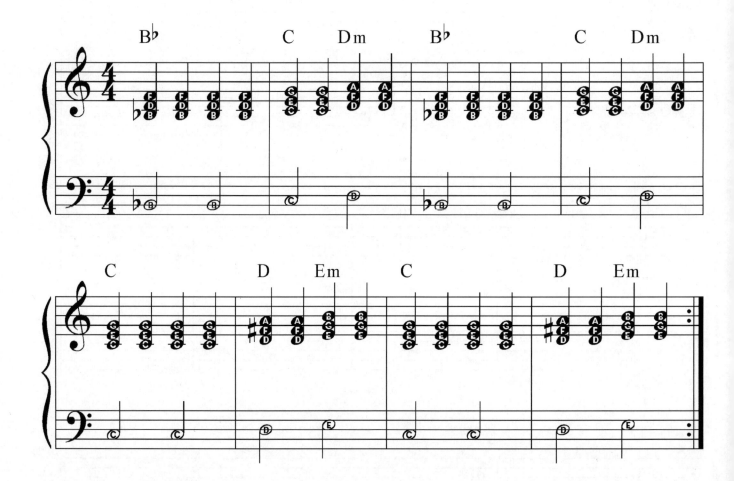

Borrowed chords are chords that don't fit into the original key of the song but using them does not mean that the song has changed key. Instead, the new chords are *borrowed* from other keys. Borrowed chords are not marked in any special way in a lead sheet, and you don't need to identify them as borrowed chords to play them correctly.

The following short example is in the key of G Major and contains two borrowed chords: D minor and C minor.

Example 12g:

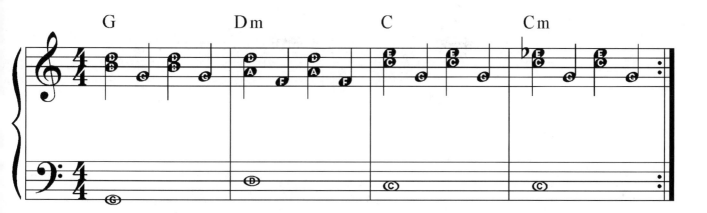

Let's play a longer song using borrowed chords. Examples 12g and 12h both contain a minor iv chord. While the IV chord is usually major in a major key, changing it to a minor chord creates a beautiful effect that is very popular with songwriters.

This next example uses the borrowed minor iv chord, most of the types of chords you have learned in this book, a modified waltz accompaniment, and a slash chord bass line. Take your time learning the notes, then play along with the recording and enjoy making music!

Example 12h:

Congratulations, you've reached the end of the book.

But this is just the beginning of your journey playing piano chords. As always, feel free to return to previous lessons to gain more experience, and don't be afraid to experiment with what you have learned to make the music your own. The techniques in this book can be combined in countless ways to play your favorite songs and your own music. Have fun!

Made in the USA
Las Vegas, NV
02 November 2024

11035117R00057